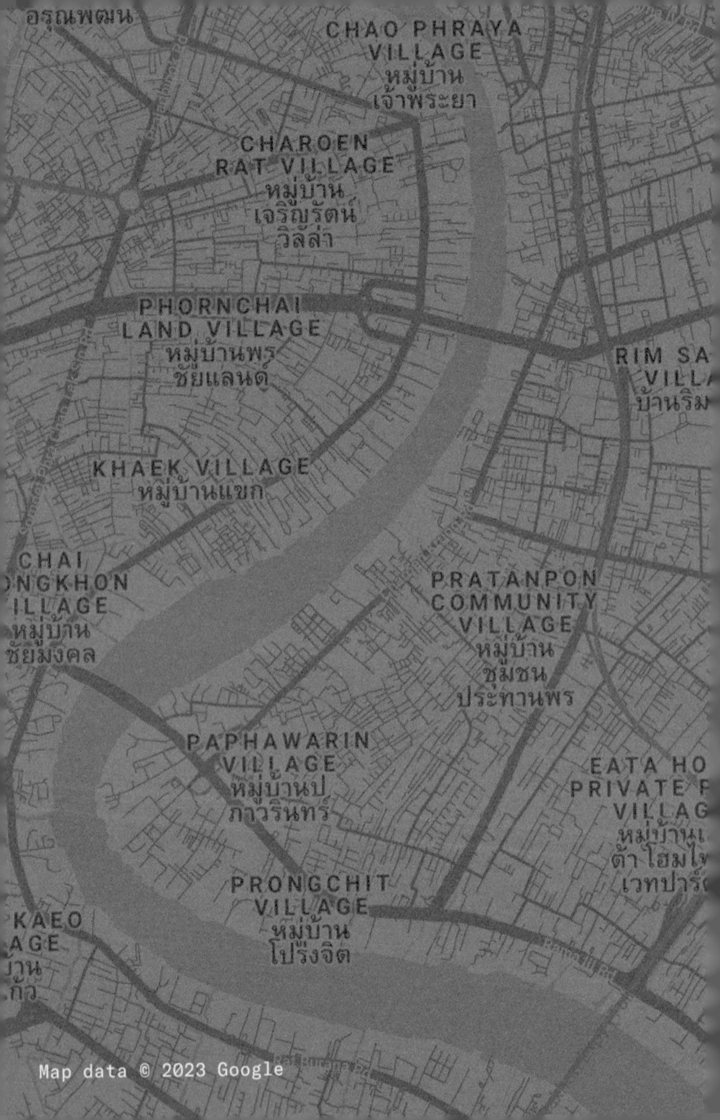
CHAO PHRAYA
VILLAGE
หมู่บ้าน
เจ้าพระยา
CHAROEN
RAT VILLAGE
หมู่บ้าน
เจริญรัตน์
วิลล่า
PHORNCHAI
LAND VILLAGE
หมู่บ้านพร
ชัยแลนด์
KHAEK VILLAGE
หมู่บ้านแขก
PRATANPON
COMMUNITY
VILLAGE
หมู่บ้าน
ชุมชน
ประทานพร
PAPHAWARIN
VILLAGE
หมู่บ้านป
ภาวรินทร์
PRONGCHIT
VILLAGE
หมู่บ้าน
โปร่งจิต
Map data © 2023 Google

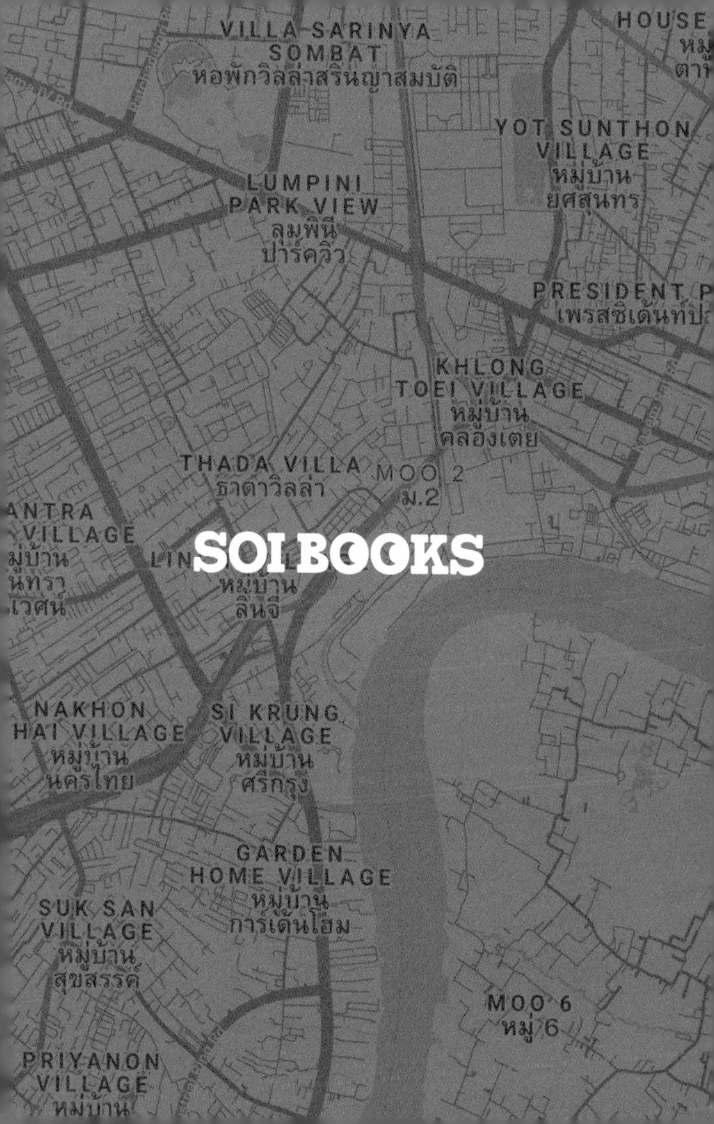
VILLA SARINYA SOMBAT
หอพักวิลล่าสรินญาสมบัติ
YOT SUNTHON VILLAGE
หมู่บ้าน
ยศสุนทร
LUMPINI PARK VIEW
ลุมพินี
ปาร์ควิว
KHLONG TOEI VILLAGE
หมู่บ้าน
คลองเตย
THADA VILLA
ธาดาวิลล่า
MOO 2
ม.2
SOI BOOKS
หมู่บ้าน
ลินจี
SI KRUNG VILLAGE
หมู่บ้าน
ศรีกรุง
GARDEN HOME VILLAGE
หมู่บ้าน
การ์เด้นโฮม
SUK SAN VILLAGE
หมู่บ้าน
สุขสรรค์
MOO 6
หมู่ 6
PRIYANON VILLAGE
หมู่บ้าน

Soi Books / Stickerbomb Ltd

This publication has been realised exclusively with the purpose and intent of a critical and satirical documentation and discussion. The views expressed in this publication are those of the respective contributors and are not necessarily shared by the publisher and its staff.

Design and layout by Ryo Sanada,
Suridh Hassan and Chip7.
Photography by CHIP7 (@chip7land) and
Adryel Talamantes (@adryel_talamantes)

ISBN: 978-1-7397509-1-6
Printed in the U.K.

@bombstagram
www.stickerbombworld.com
www.soibooks.com

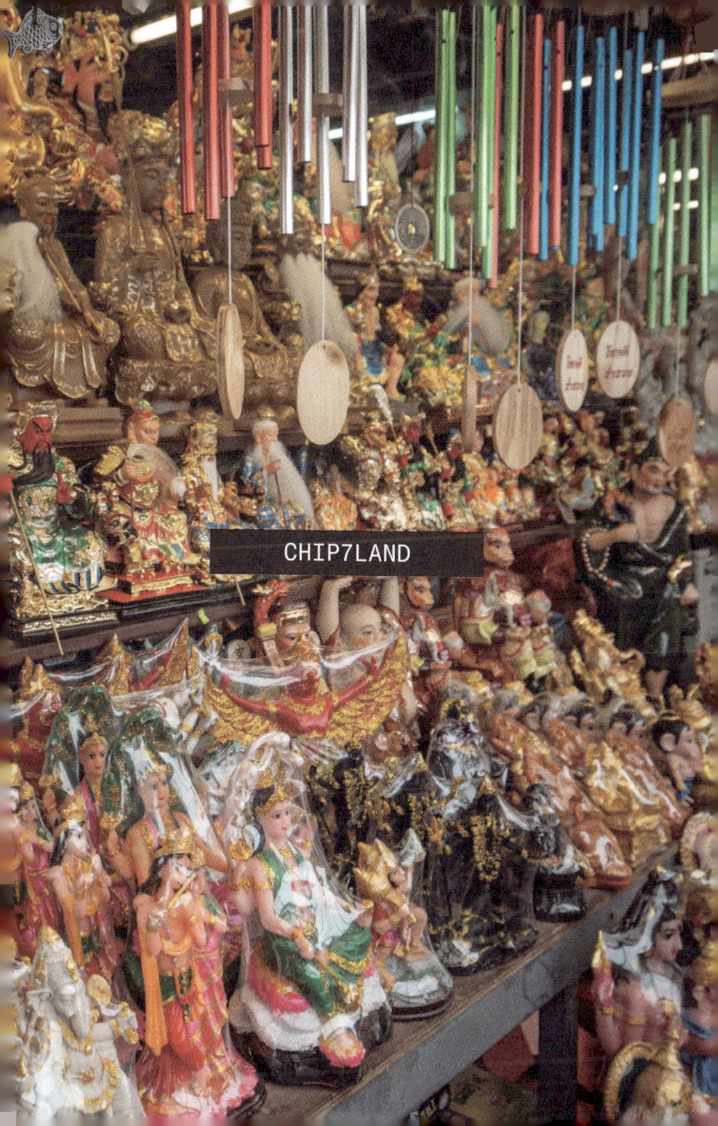
CHIP7LAND

กรุงเทพมหานคร
อมรรัตนโกสินทร์
มหินทรายุธยามหา
ดิลก ภพนพรัตน์
ราชธานีบุรีรมย์ อุดม
ราชนิเวศน์ มหา
สถาน อมรพิมาน
อวตารสถิต สักกะ
ทัตติยะวิษณุกรรม
ประสิทธิ์

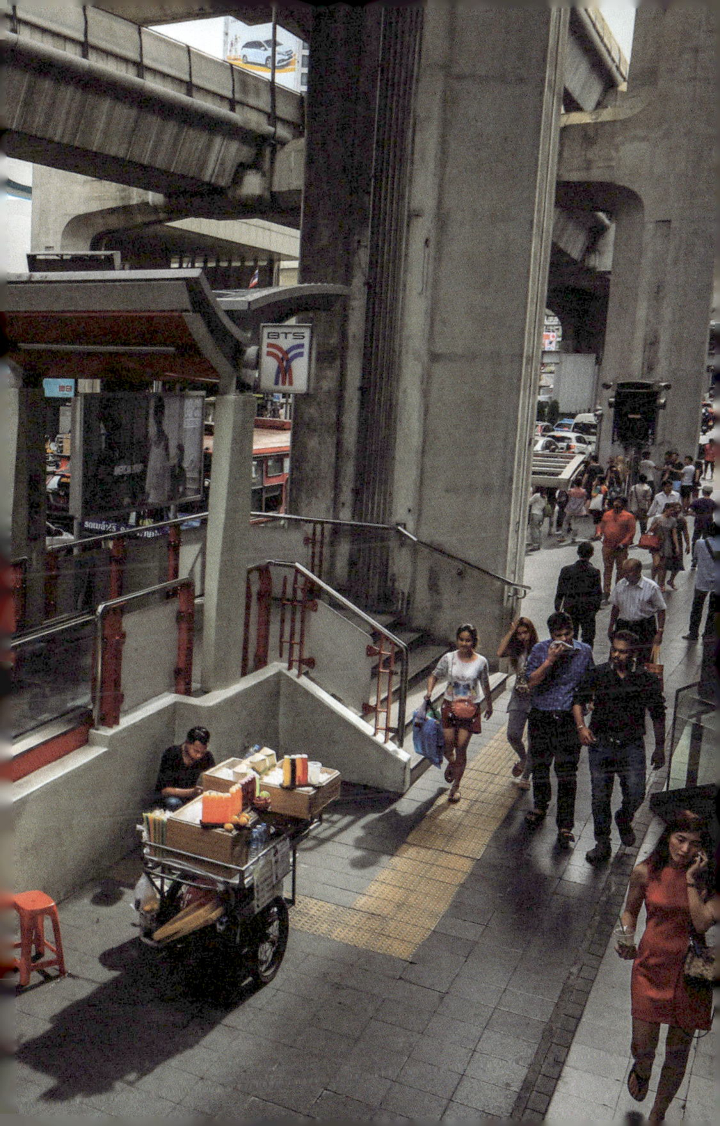
BTS

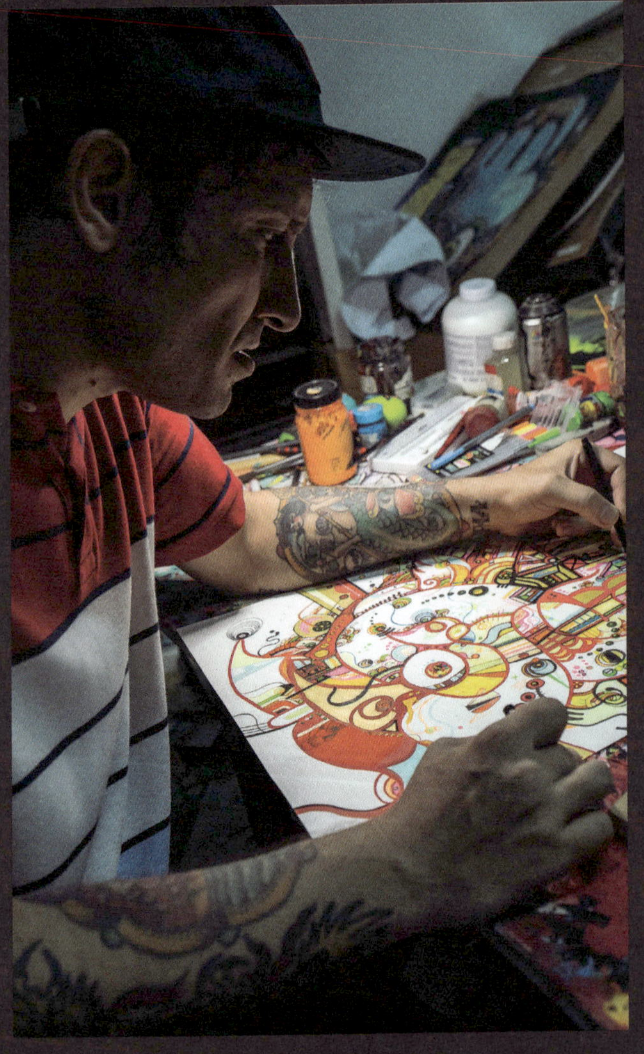

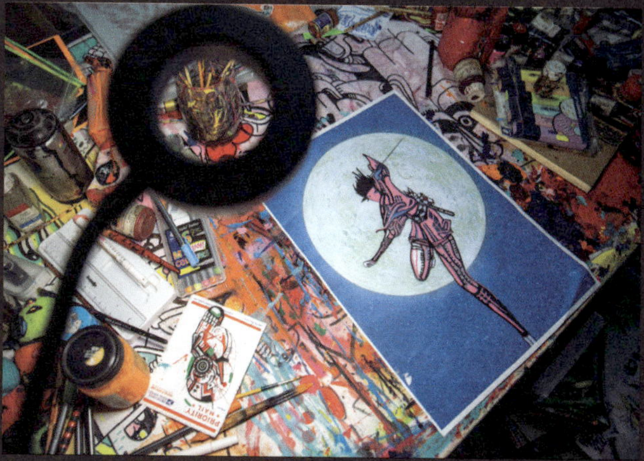

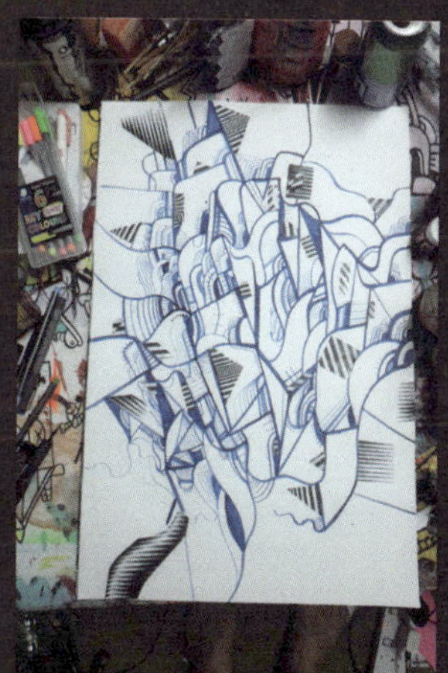

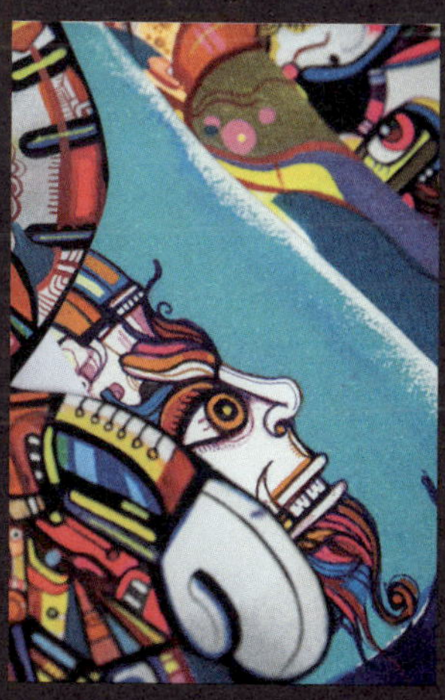

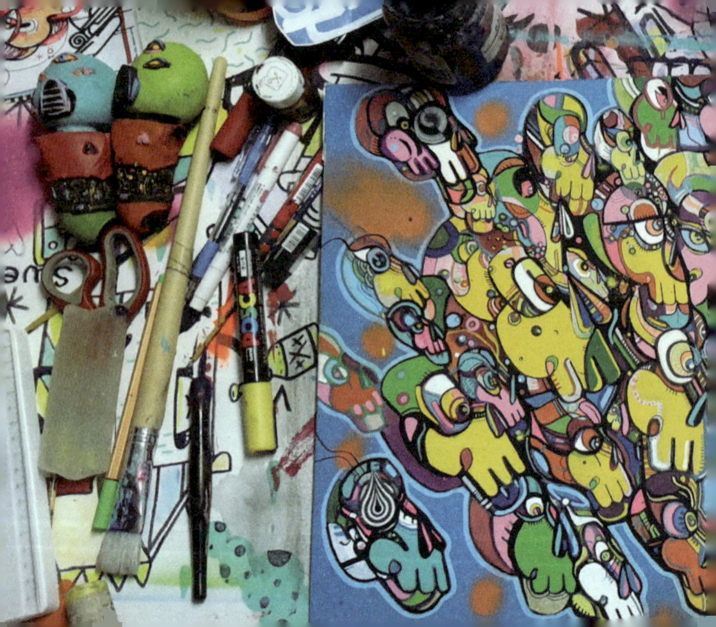

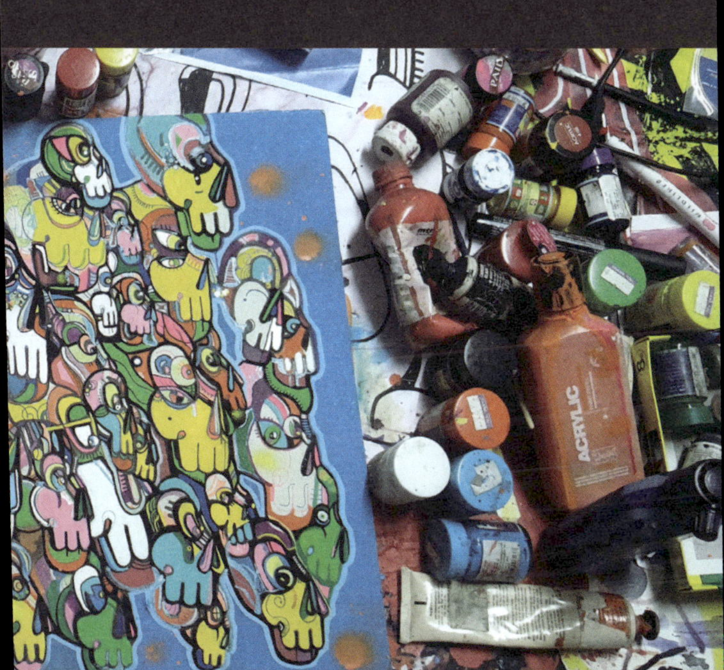
ACRYLIC

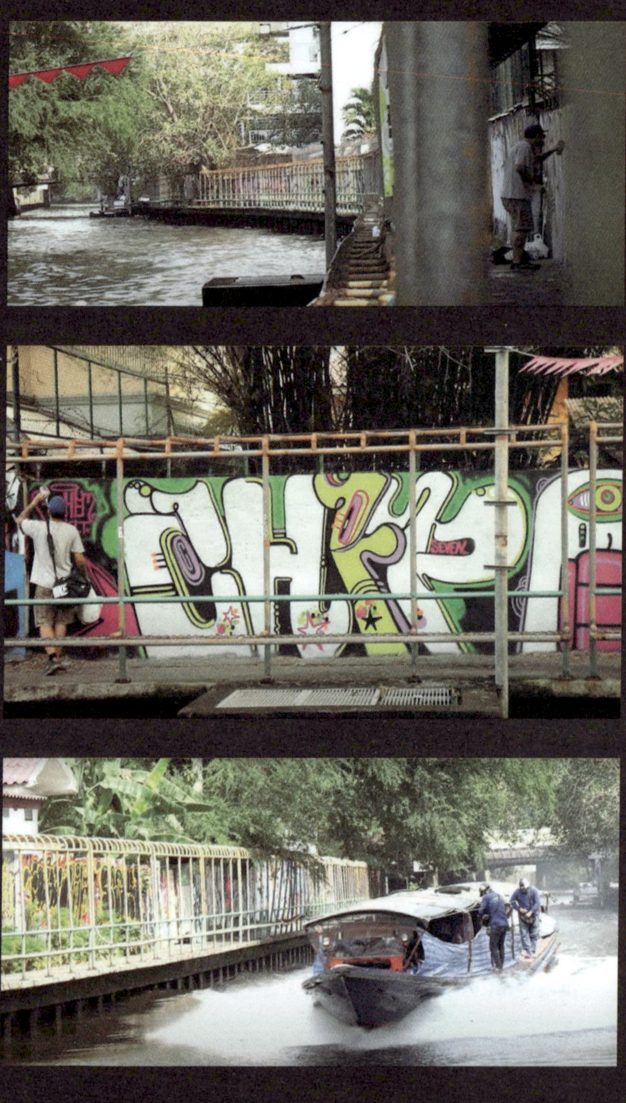
SEVEN

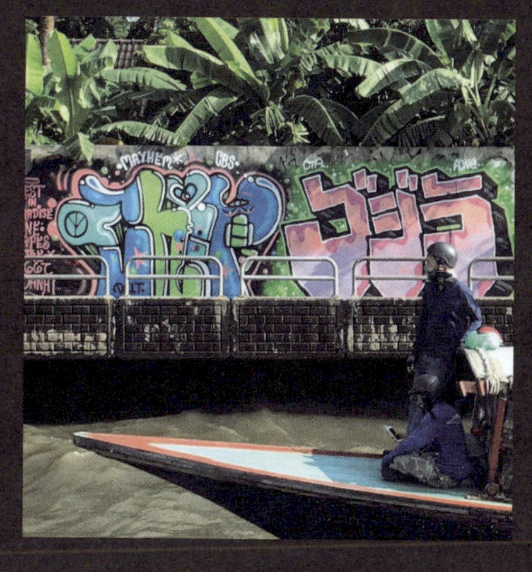
MAYHEM
CBS

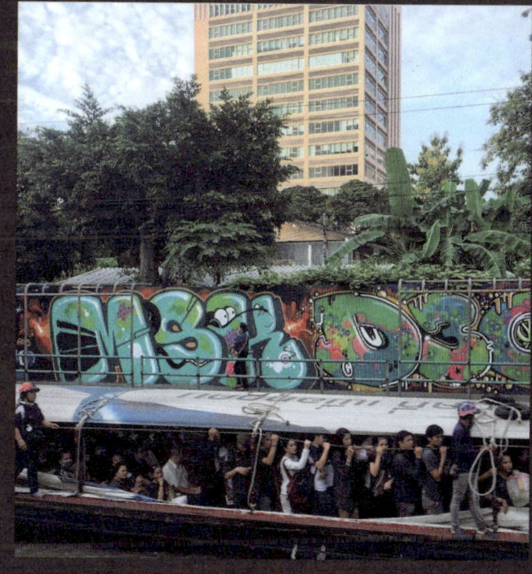

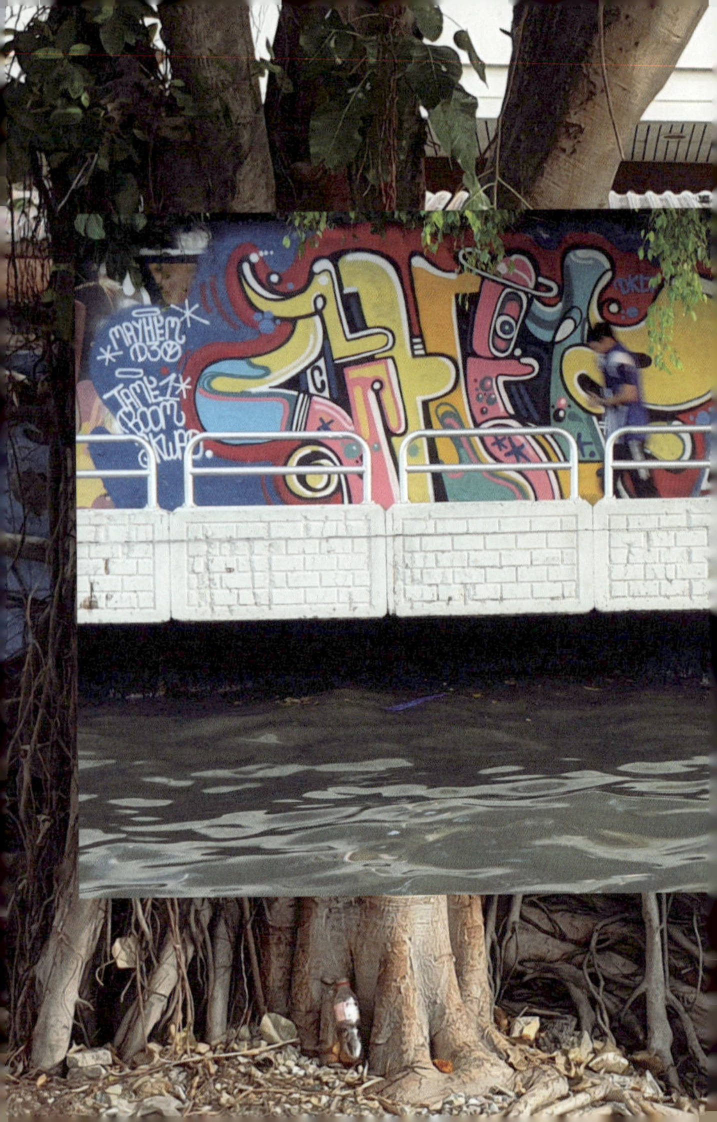
MAYHEM

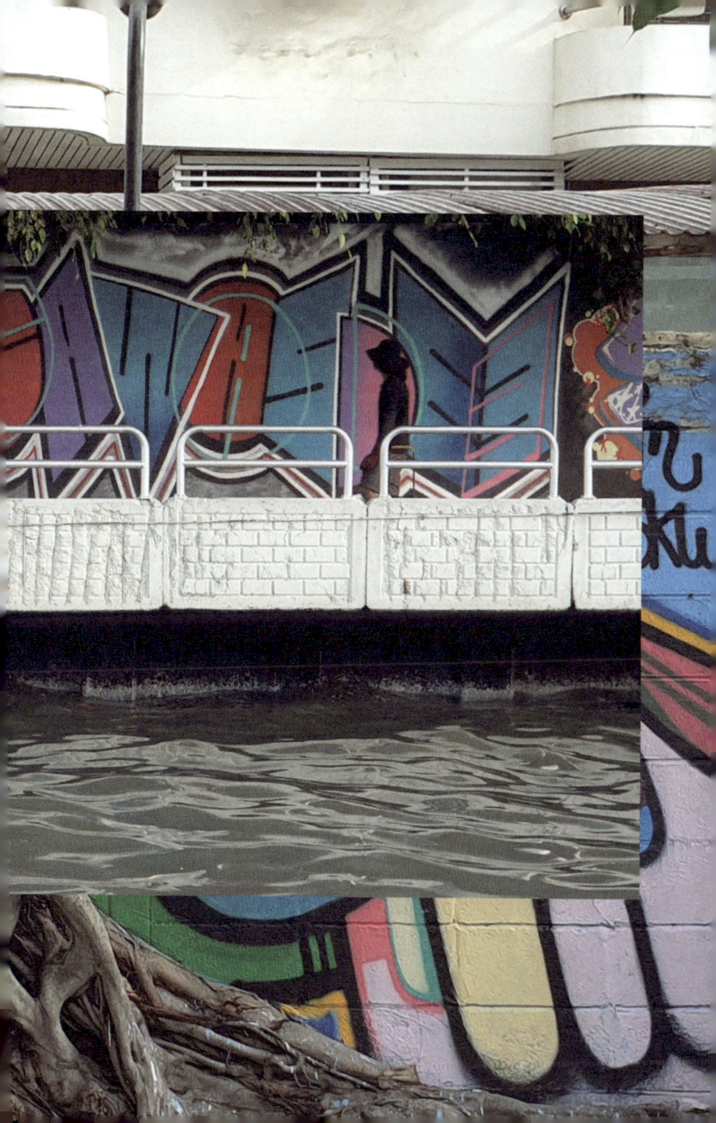

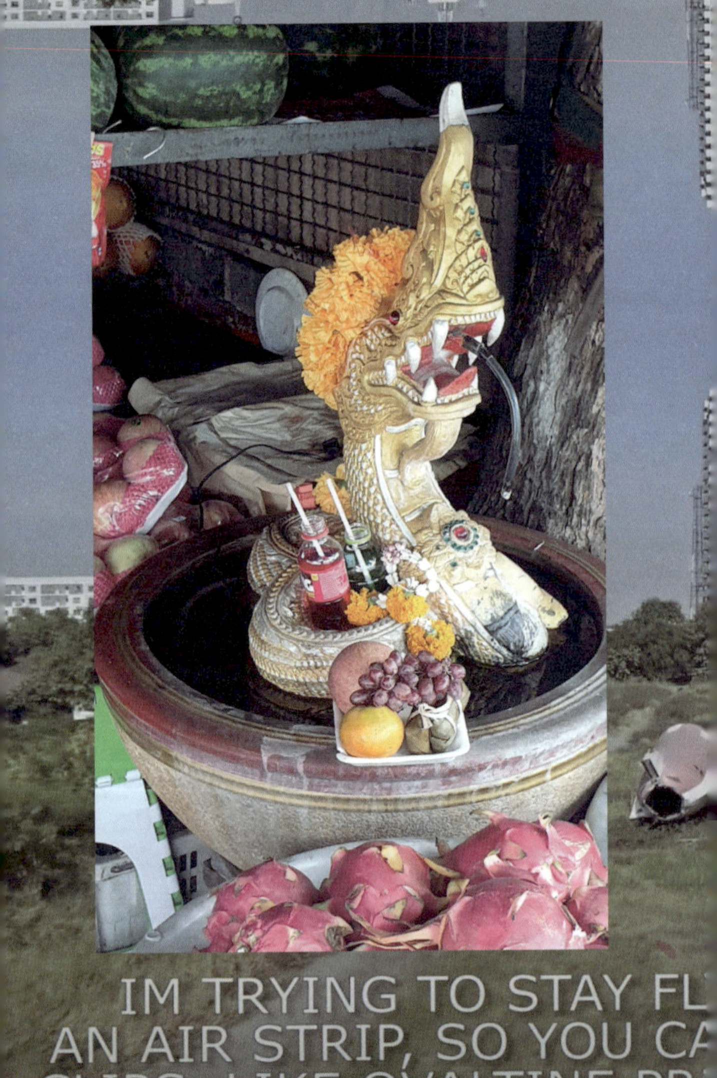

IM TRYING TO STAY FL
AN AIR STRIP, SO YOU CA
CLIPS, LIKE OVALTINE PR

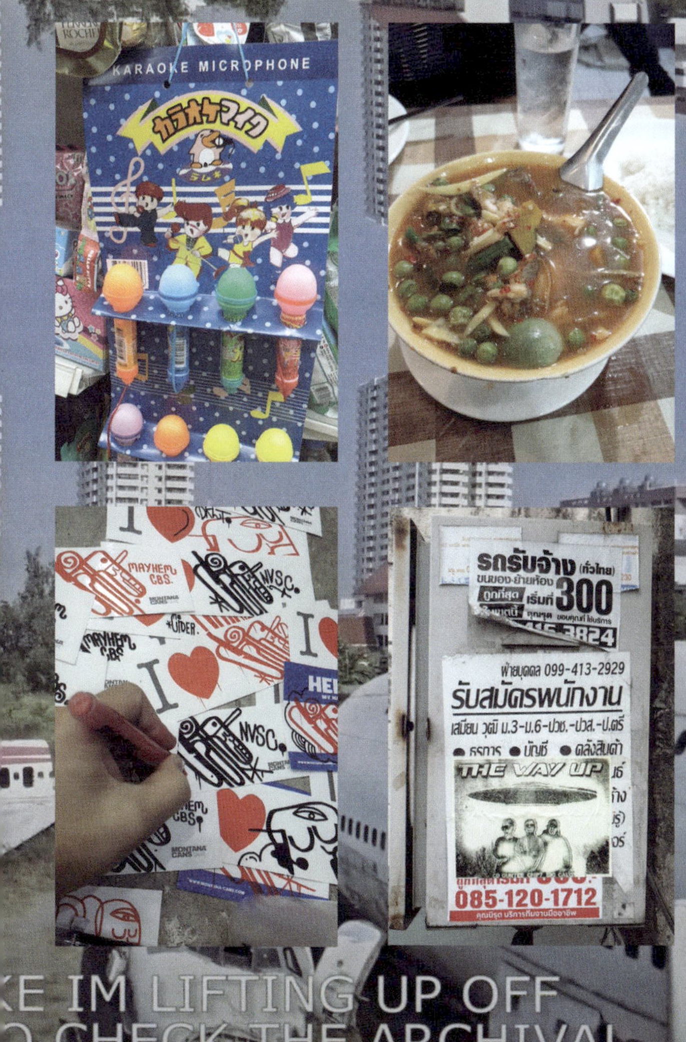

KE IM LIFTING UP OFF
O CHECK THE ARCHIVAL
ATION BACK IN THE MIX

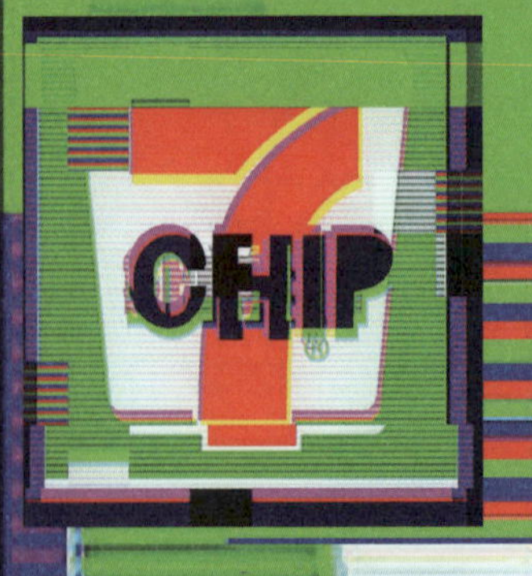

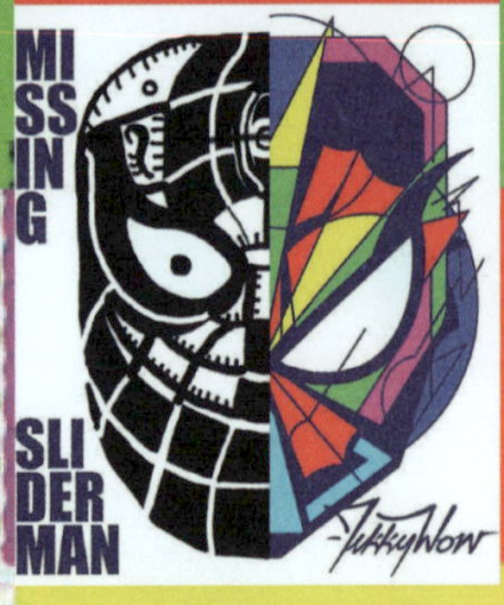

BANGKOK INVADERS

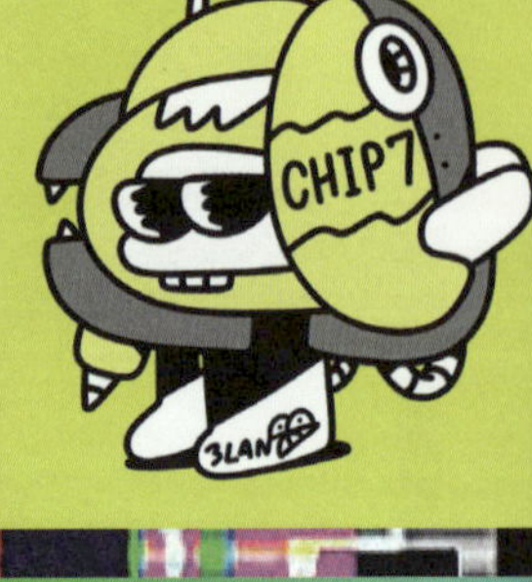

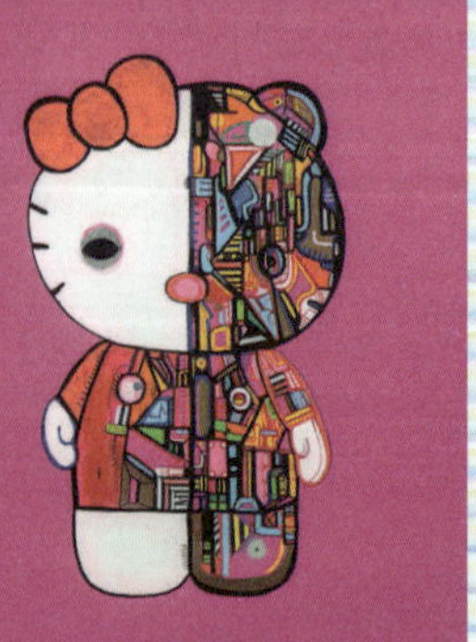

CHIP7 STILL LOVES YOU

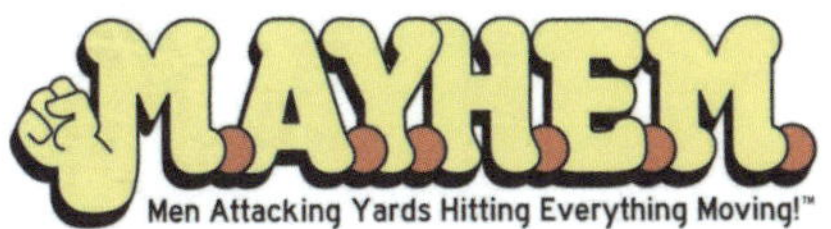

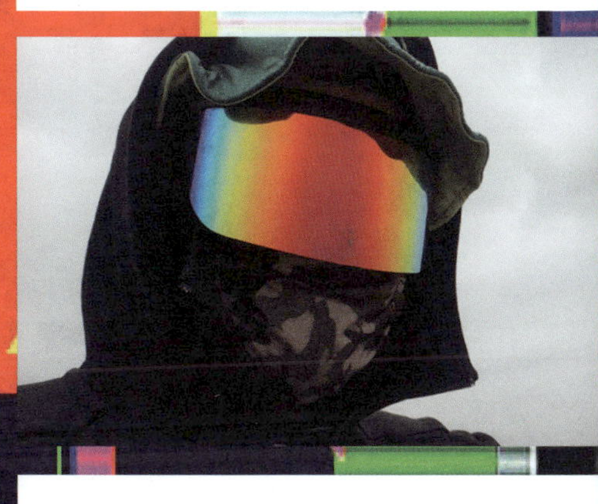

M.A.Y.H.E.M.

Men Attacking Yards Hitting Everything Moving!™

It's Computer Chip7 of the Mayhem Cru
Dirty30, Bangkok Alien also too
And that's all I hold dear
And to what I felt true

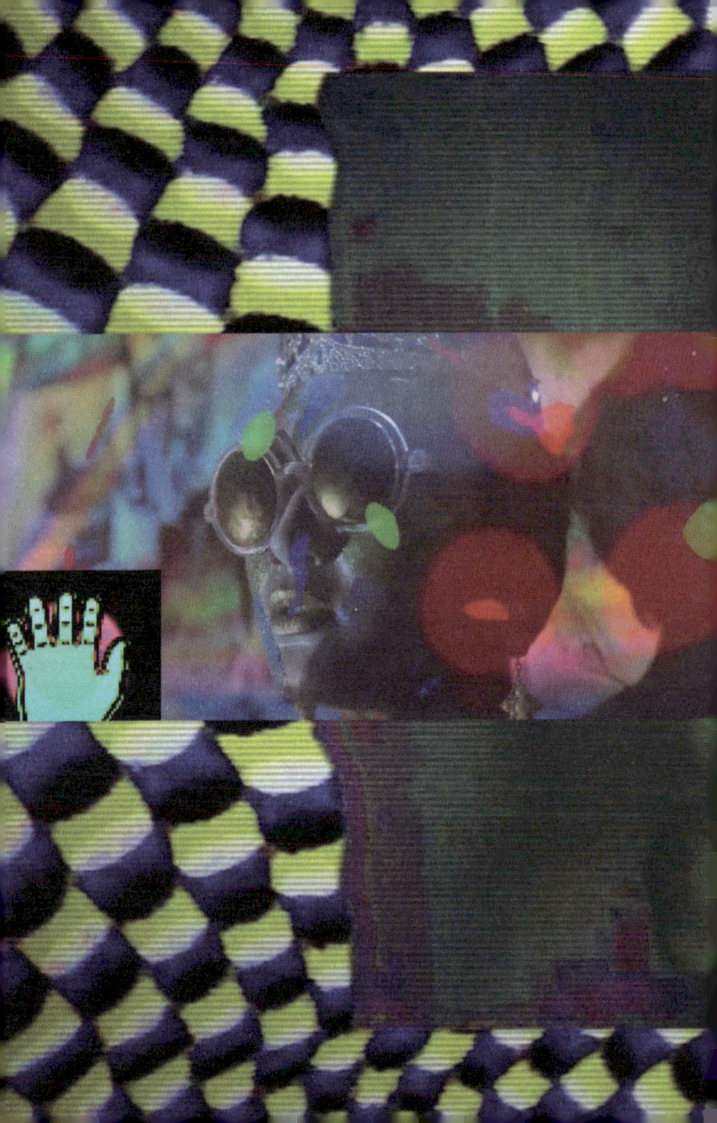

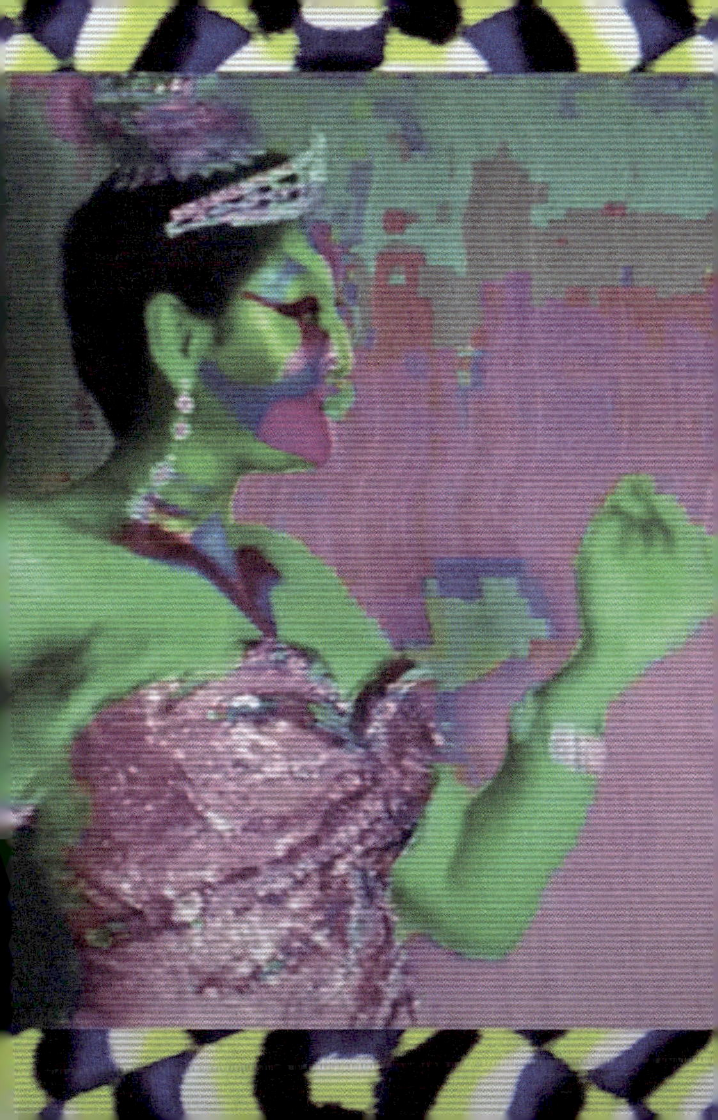

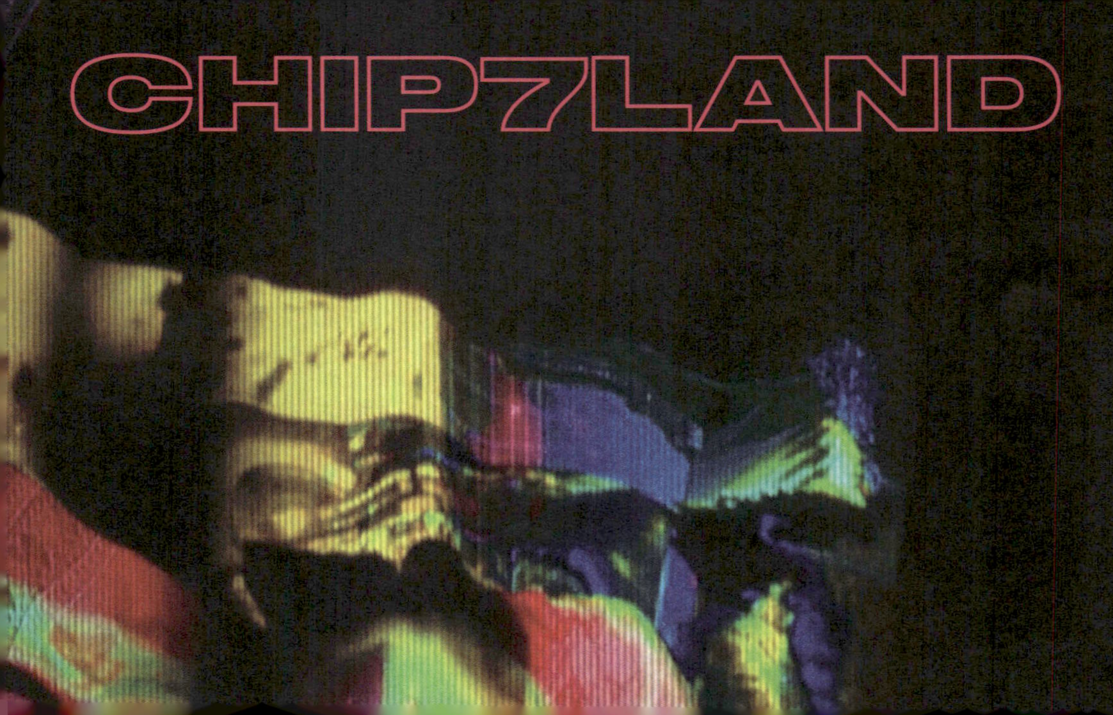
CHIP7LAND

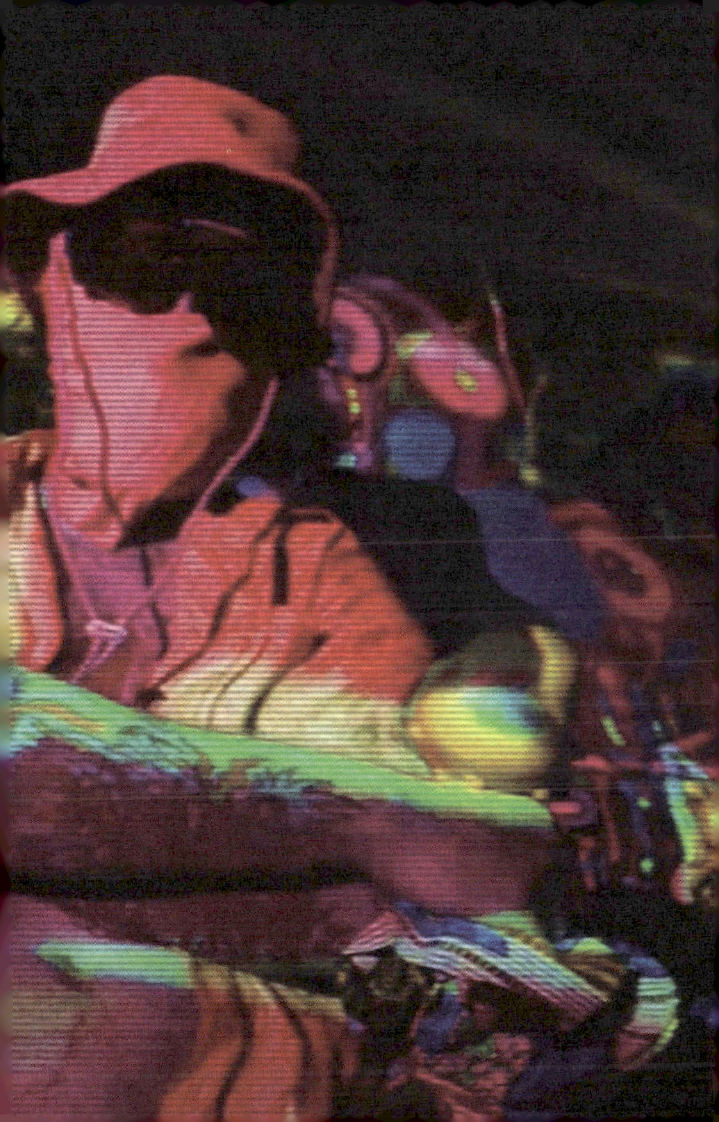

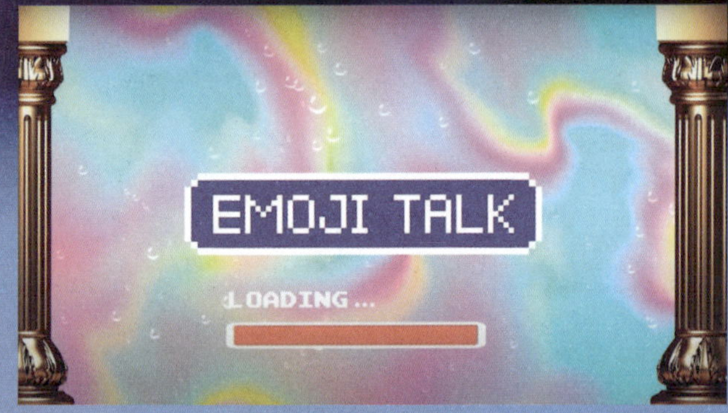
EMOJI TALK
LOADING...

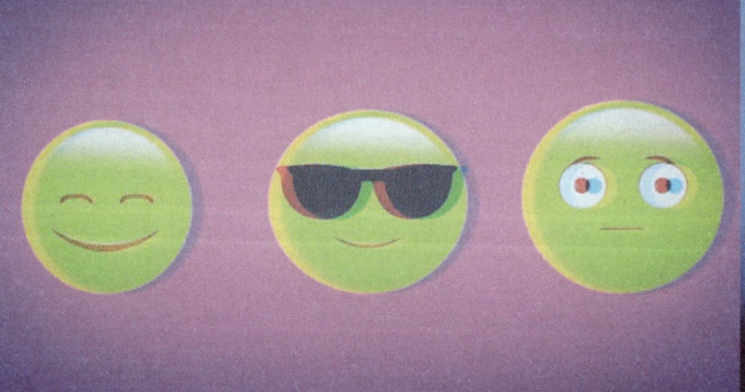

THUNDER STORM YOUR BUNKERS.SCAMBLE YOUR CLOSED CIRCUITS TRANSFORM YOUR MONSTERS TO AMPLE SOULS WITH PURPOSE

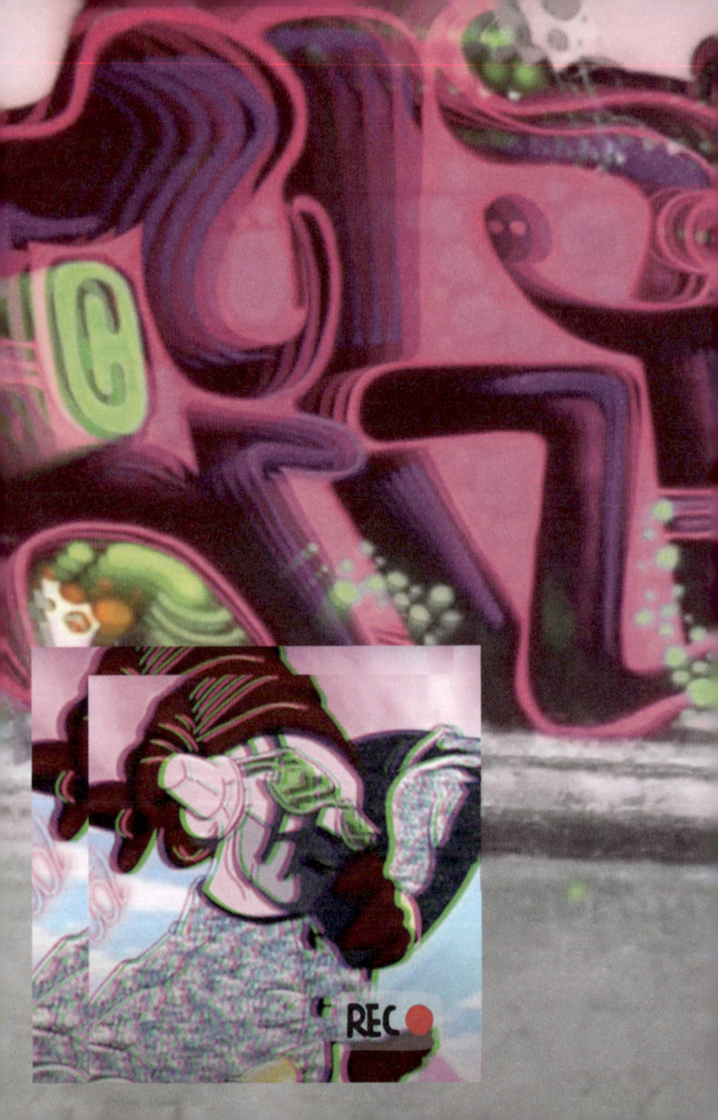
REC

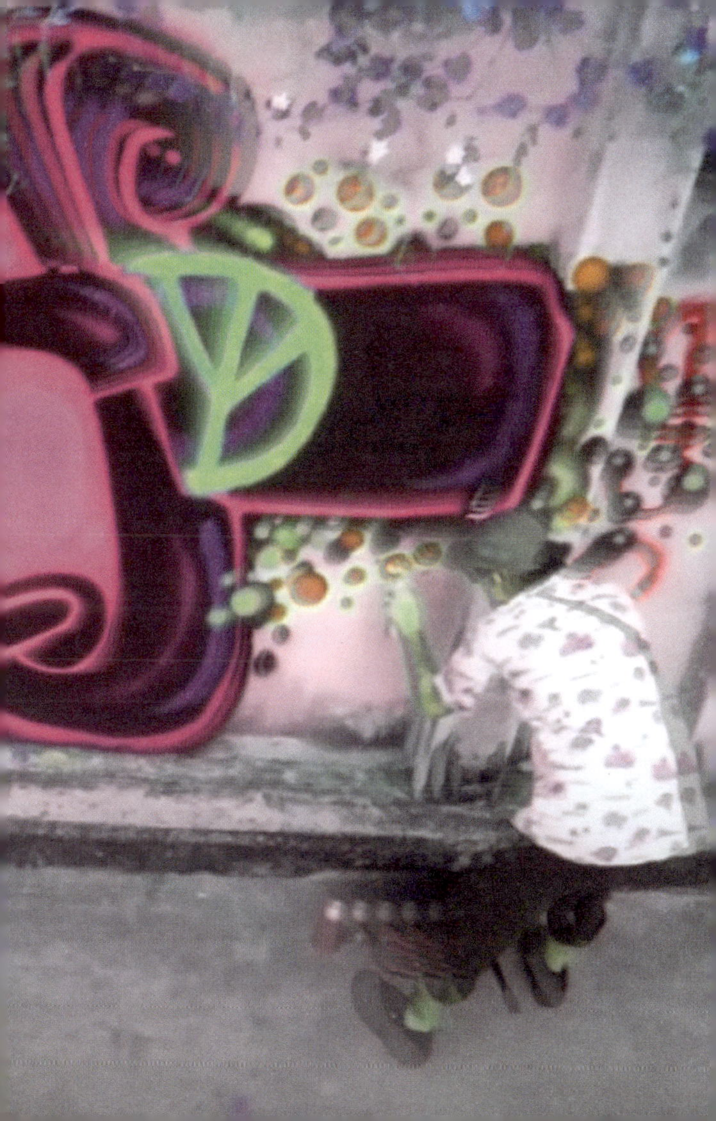

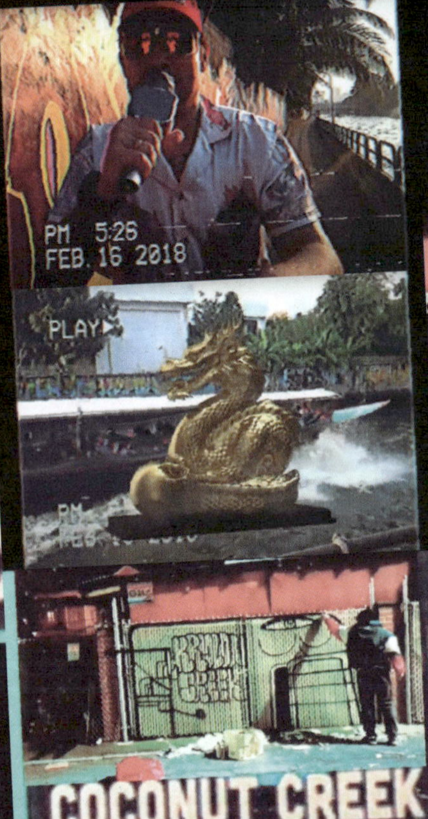
PM 5:26
FEB. 16 2018
PLAY
COCONUT CREEK

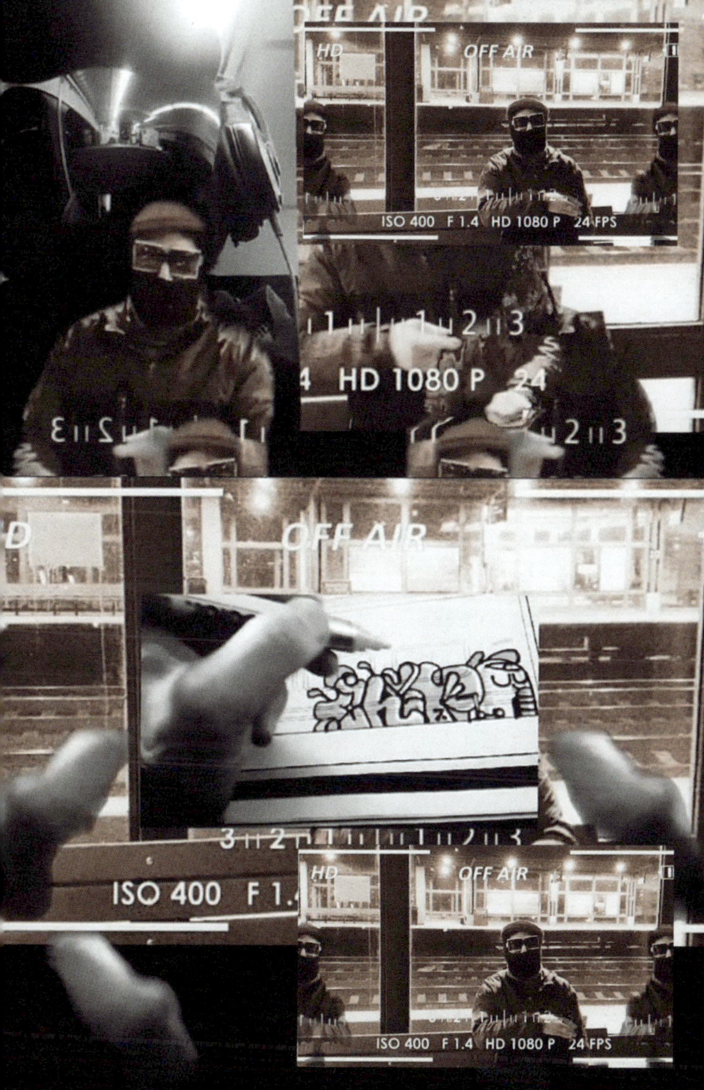

HD
OFF AIR
ISO 400 F 1.4 HD 1080 P 24 FPS
HD 1080 P
OFF AIR
ISO 400 F 1.4
HD
OFF AIR
ISO 400 F 1.4 HD 1080 P 24 FPS

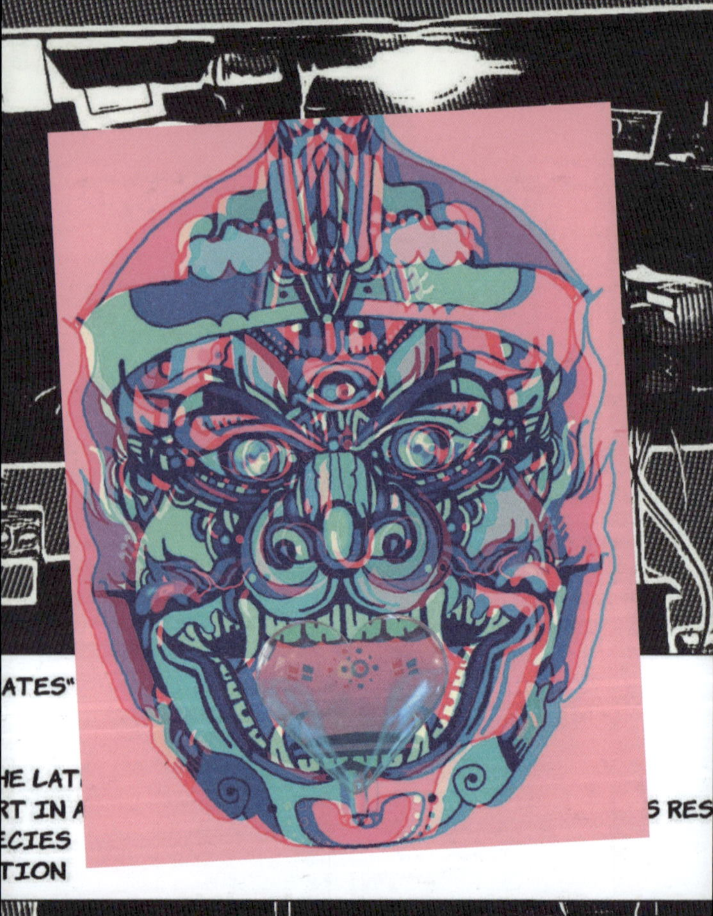
ATES"
HE LAT
RT IN A
S RES
ECIES
TION

BIONIC
PROPHET TO
CONQUER WITH
MATHMATIKS.
THE TRIBAL
ANTITOXIN
DEBOXING
EVERY
SAVAGE.

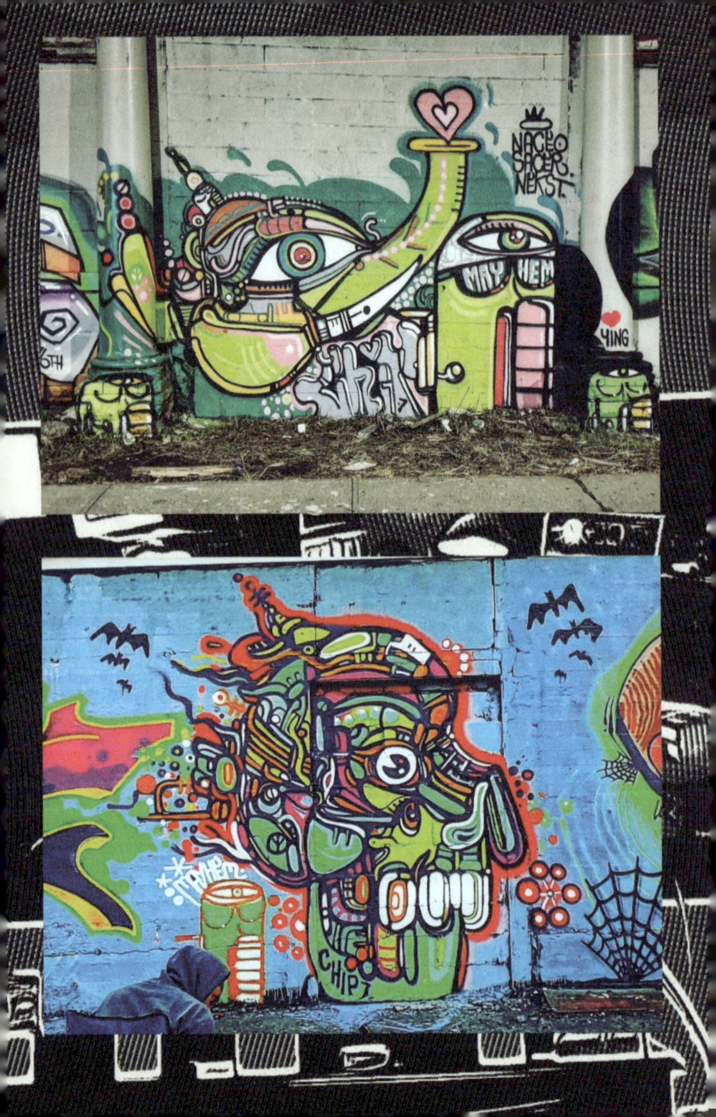
NACHO
SACER.
NEKST.
MAY HEM
YING

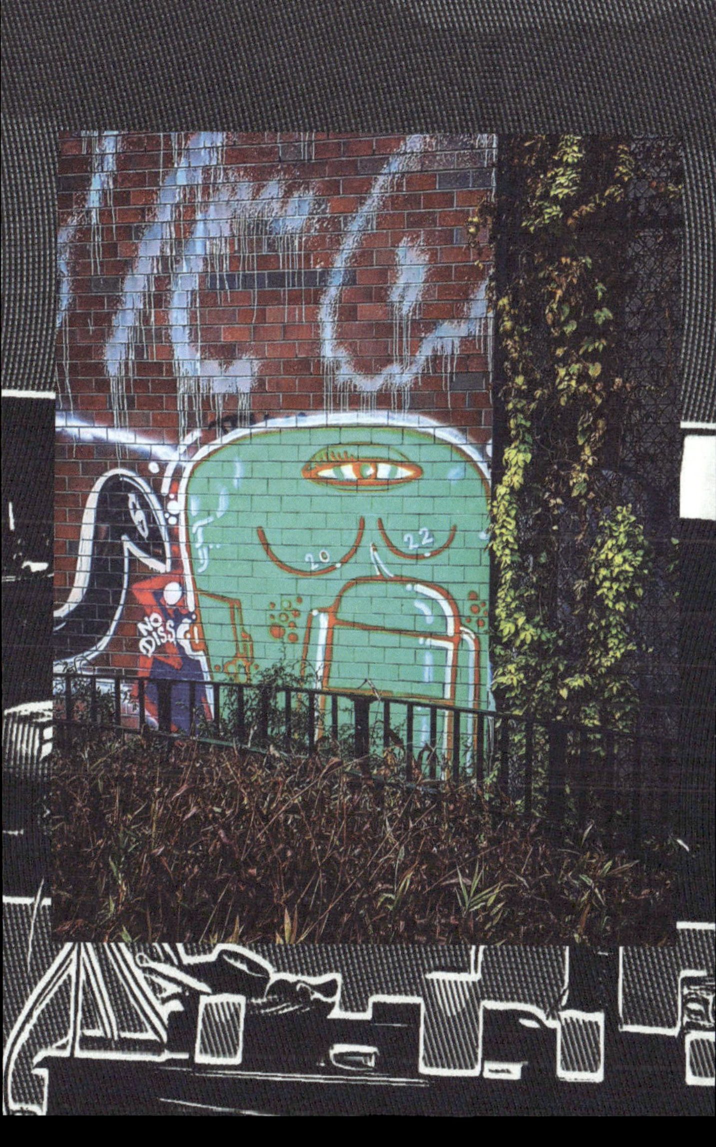
NO DISS

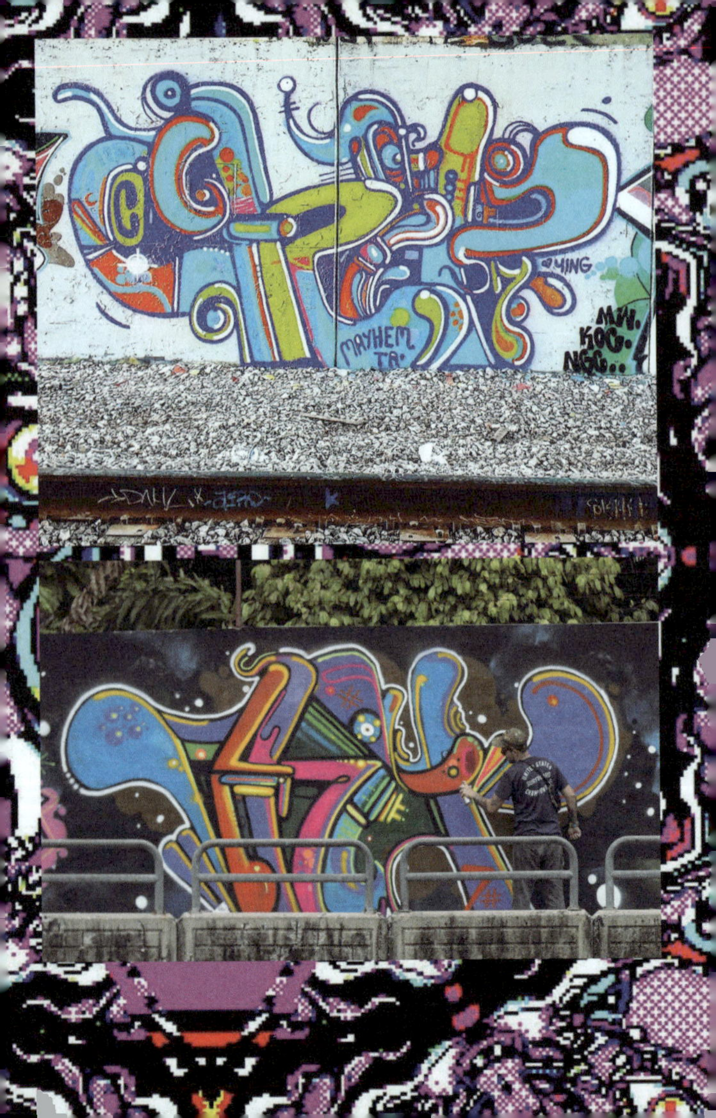
MAYHEM
TR.
MW.
KOG.
NGC..

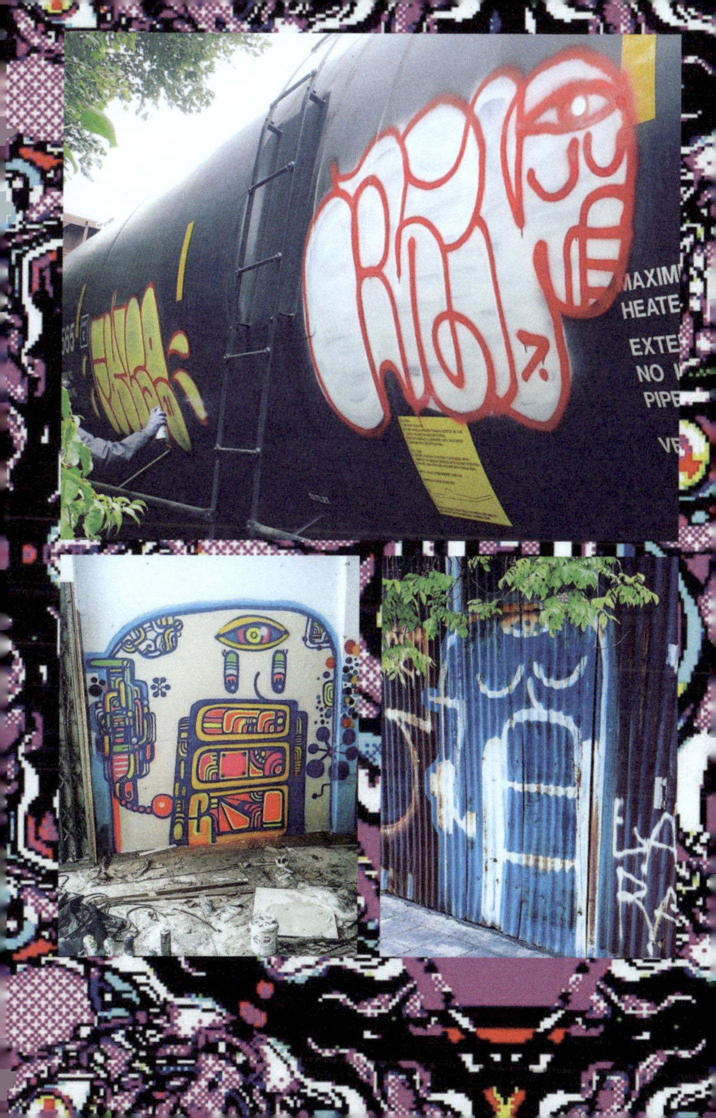

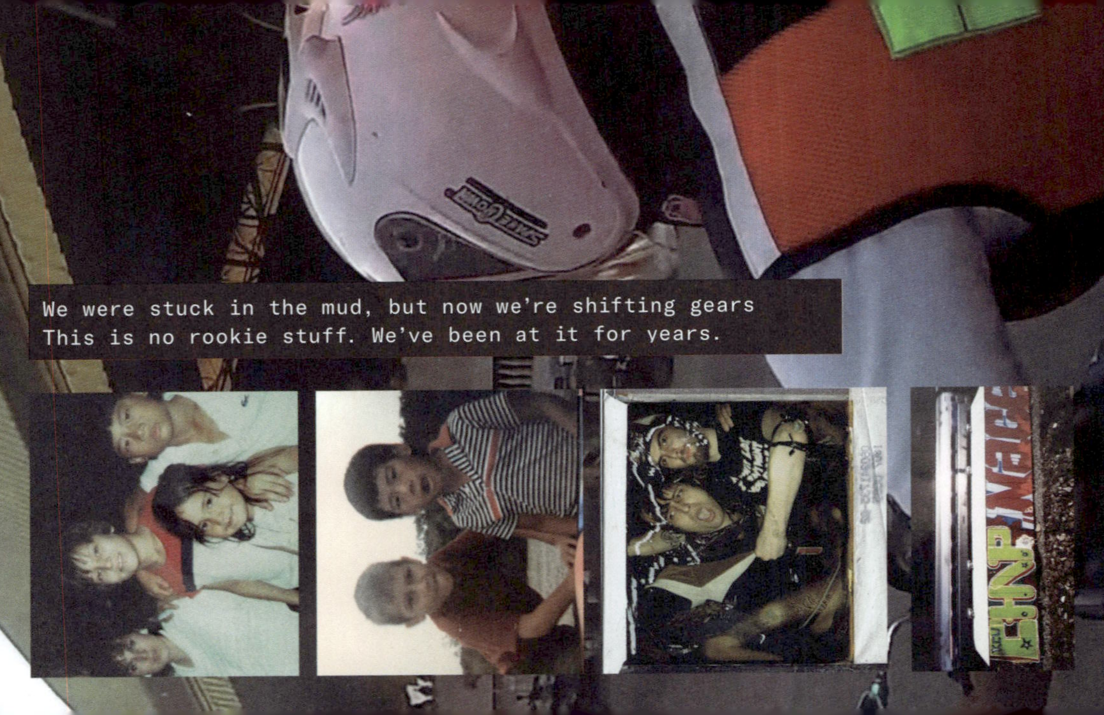

We were stuck in the mud, but now we're shifting gears
This is no rookie stuff. We've been at it for years.

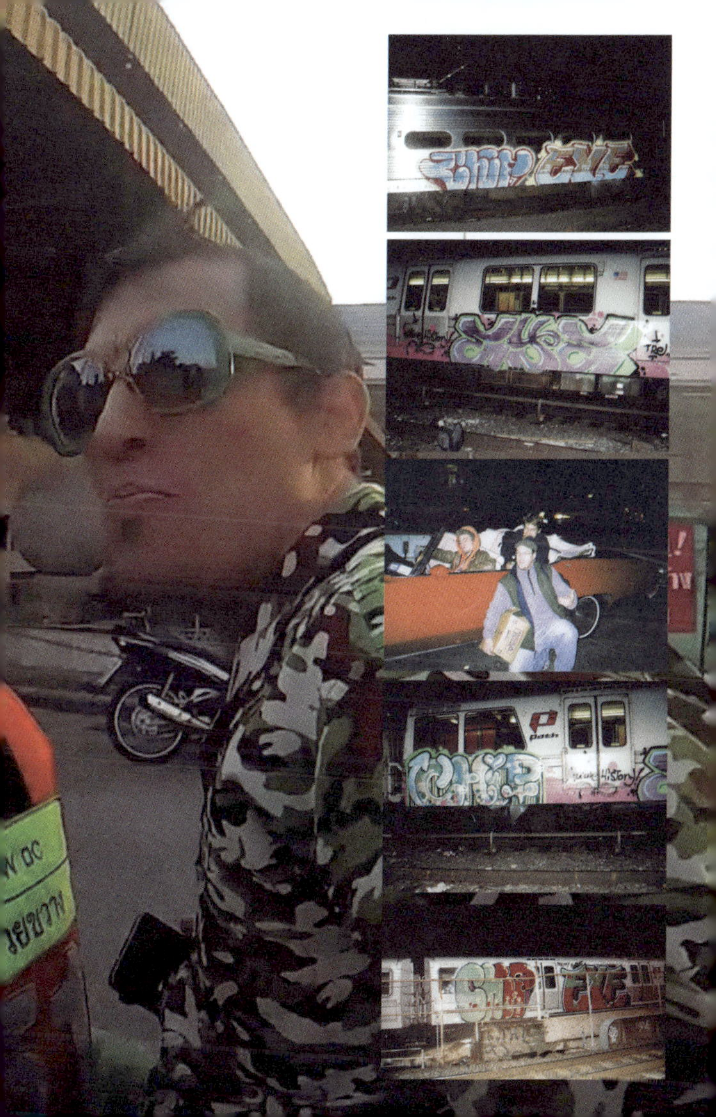

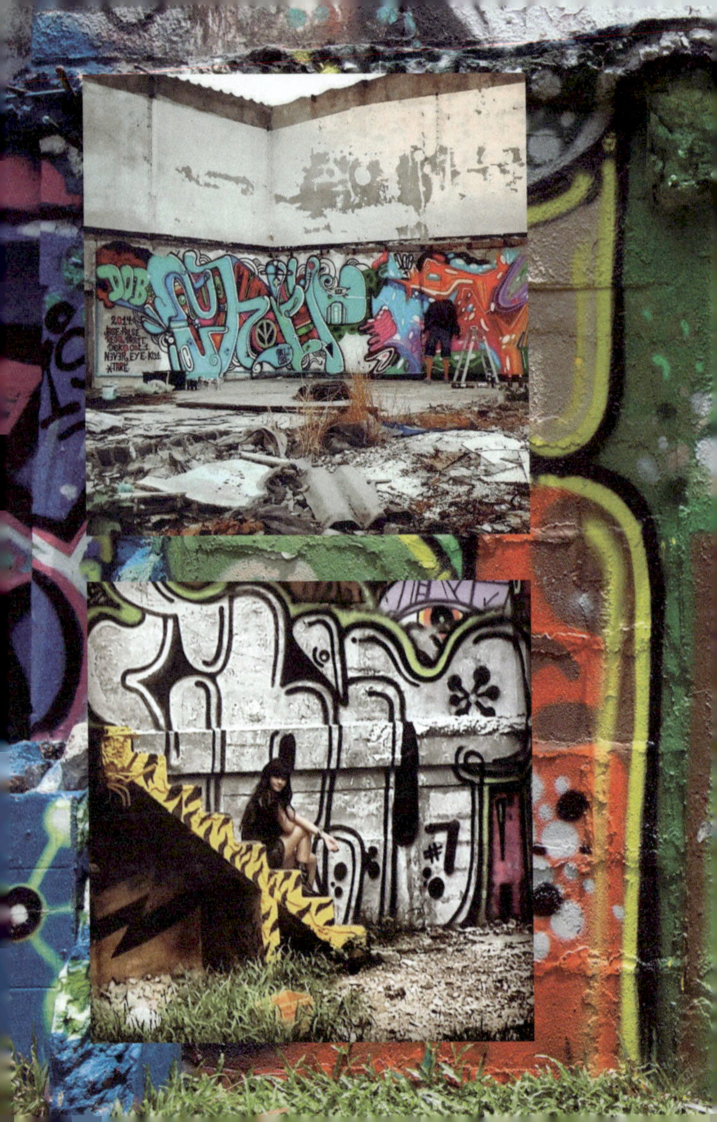
DOB
2014
NEVER EYE-KOI
#7

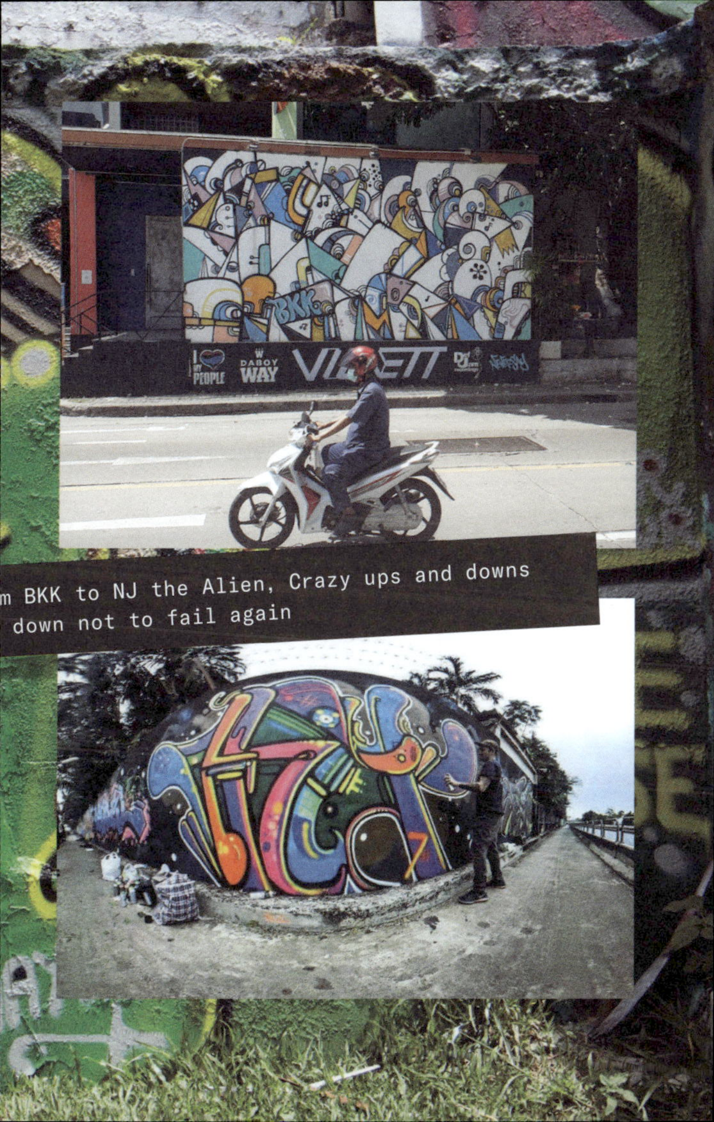
BKK
DABOY
WAY
m BKK to NJ the Alien, Crazy ups and downs
down not to fail again

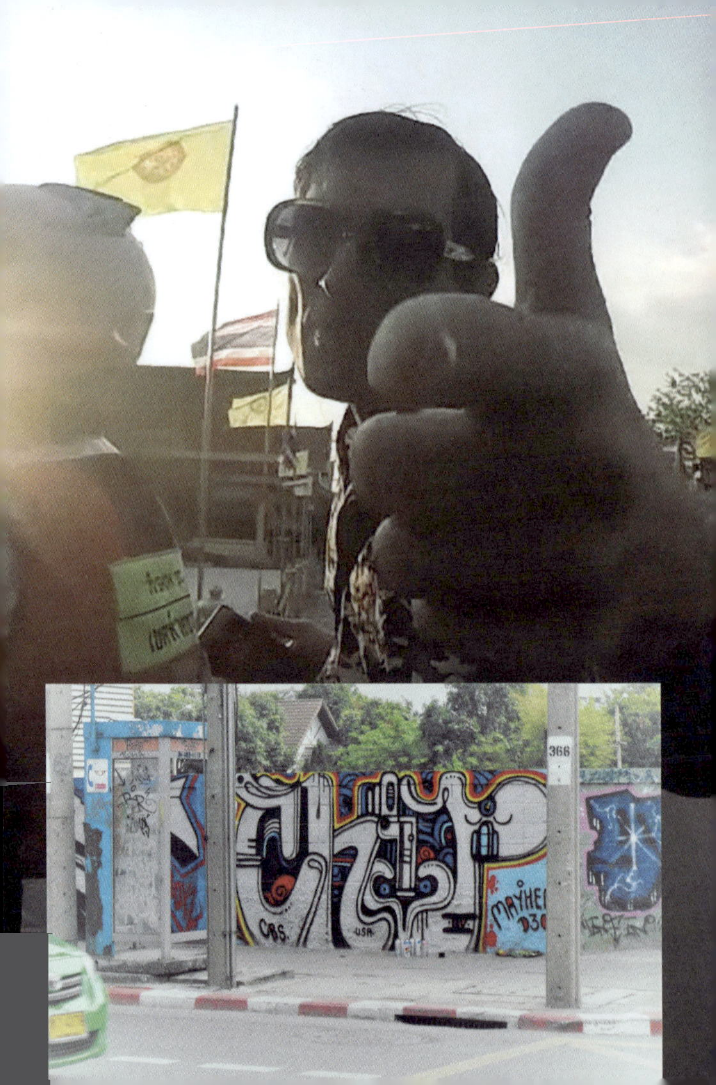
366
CBS.
USA

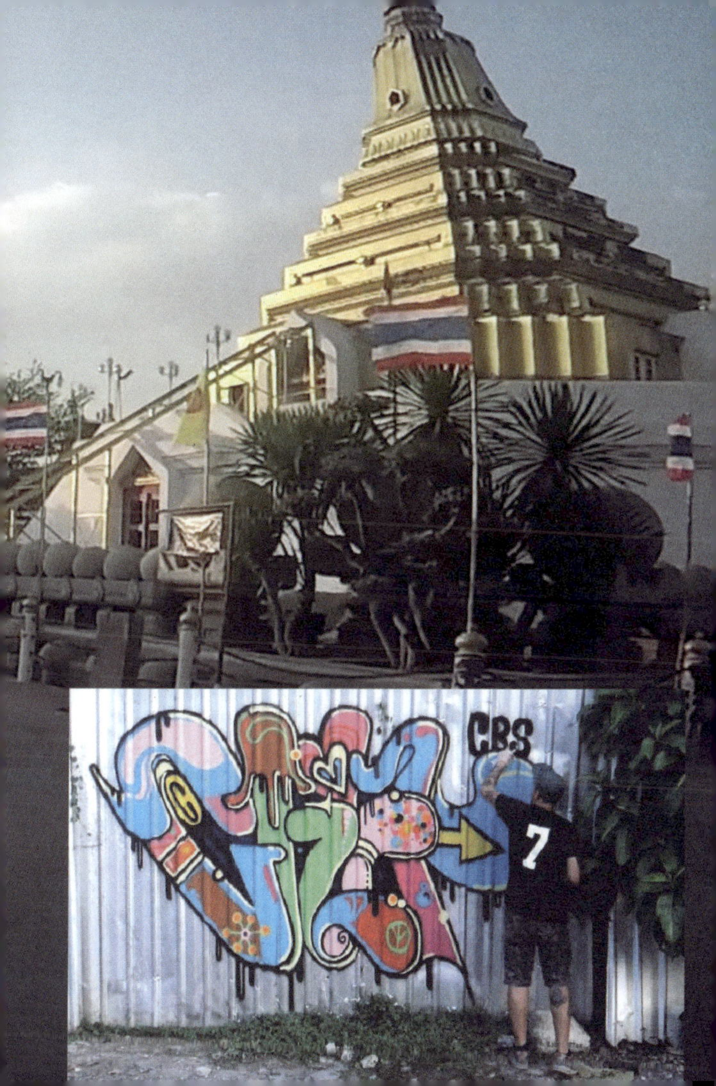
CBS
7

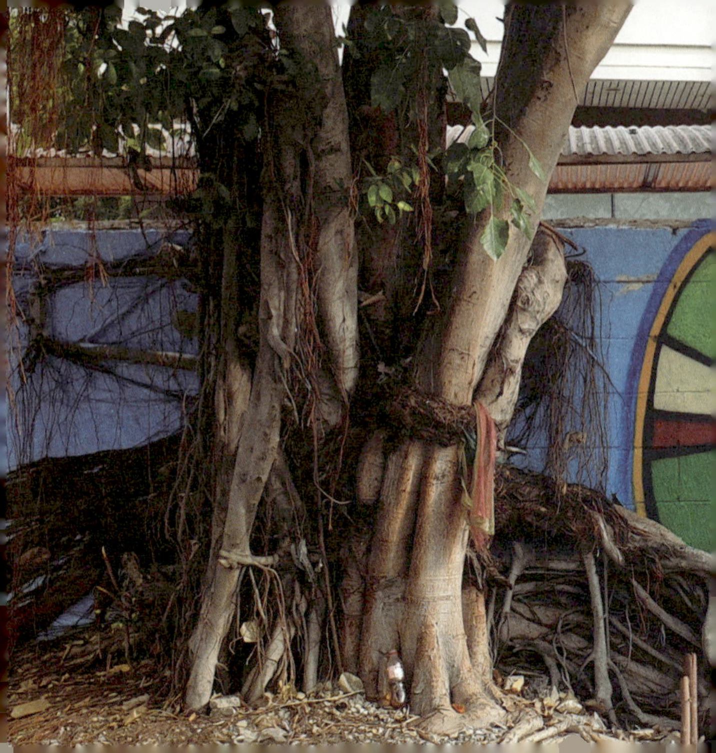

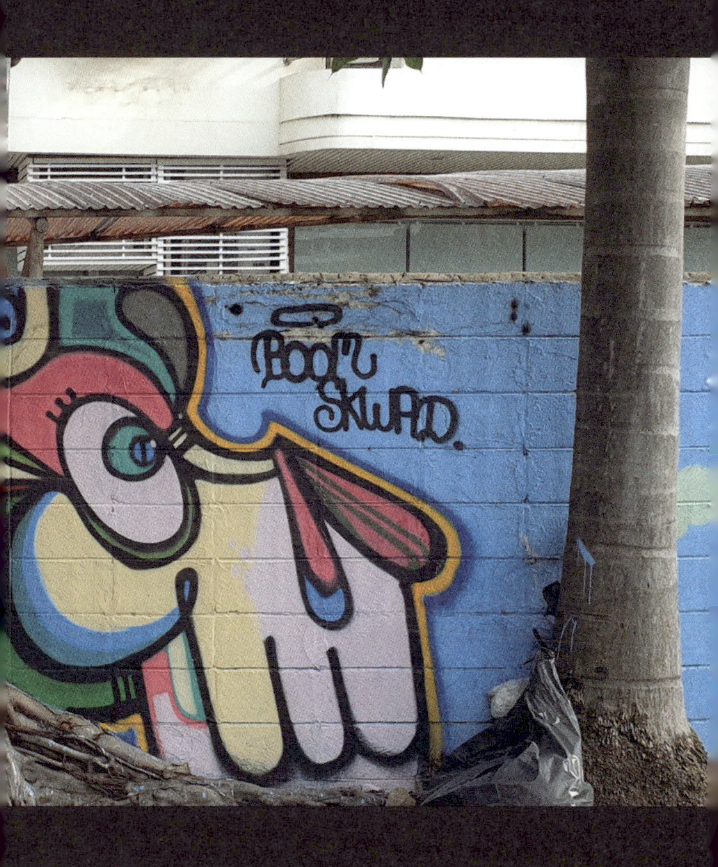

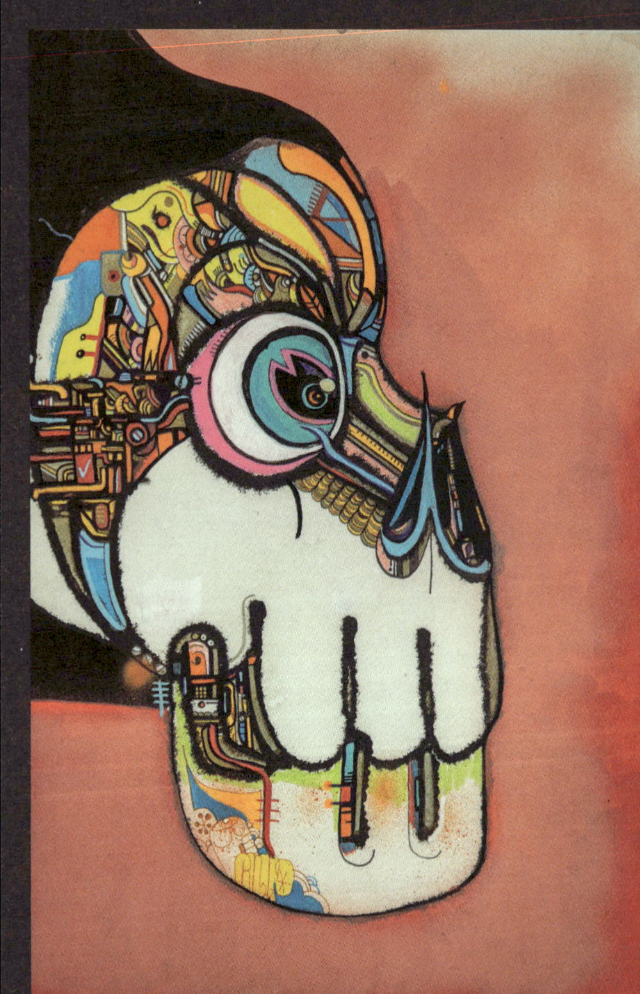

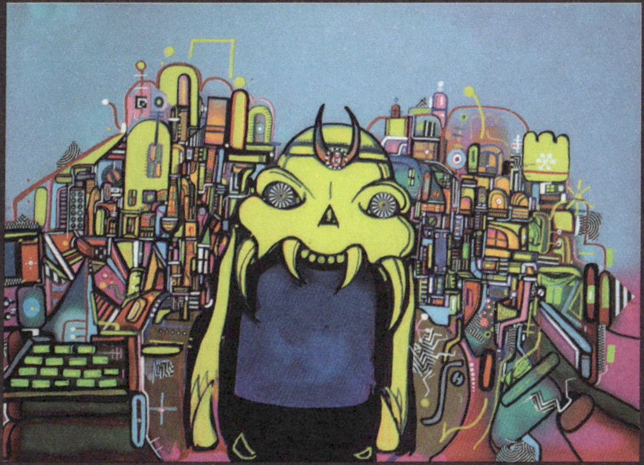

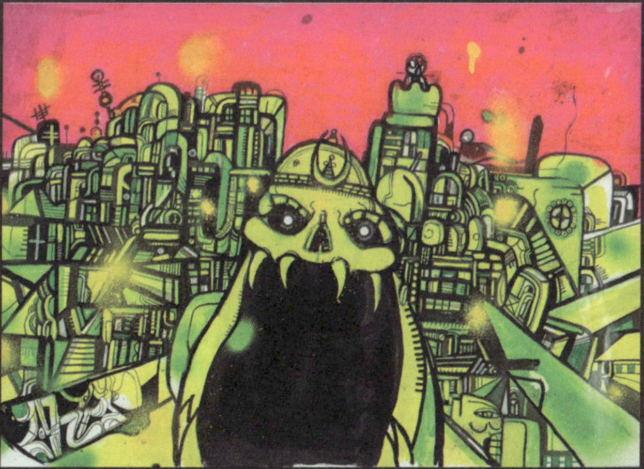

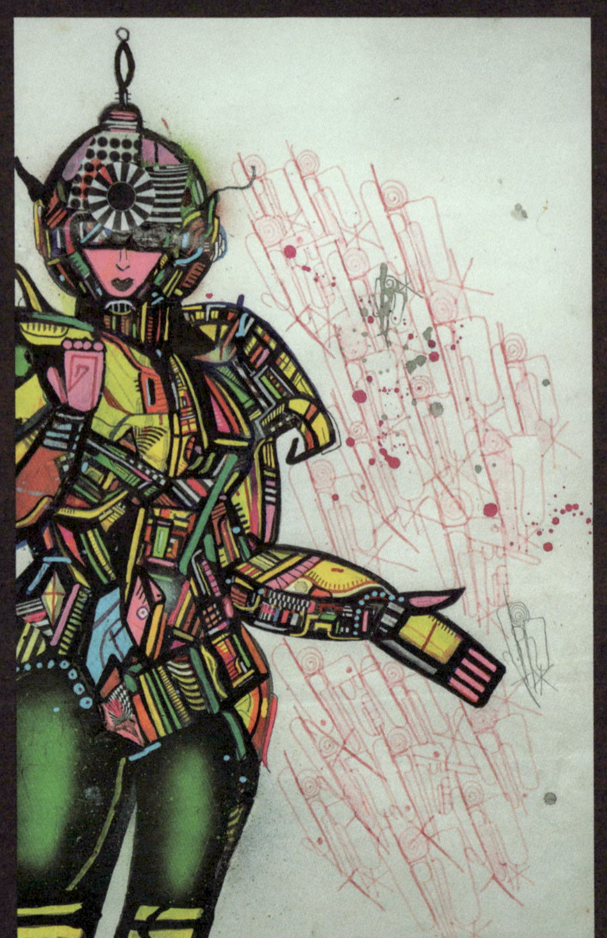

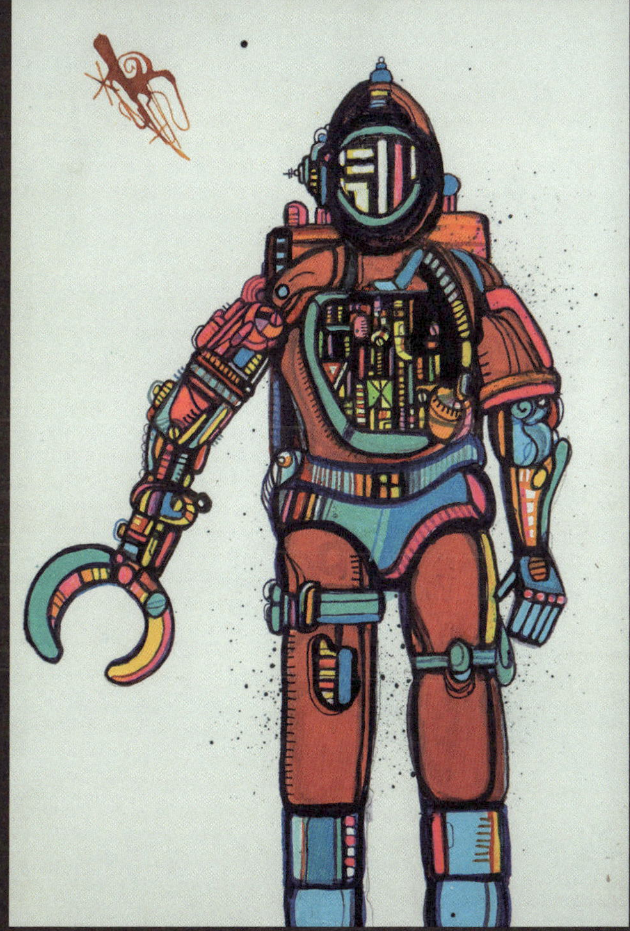

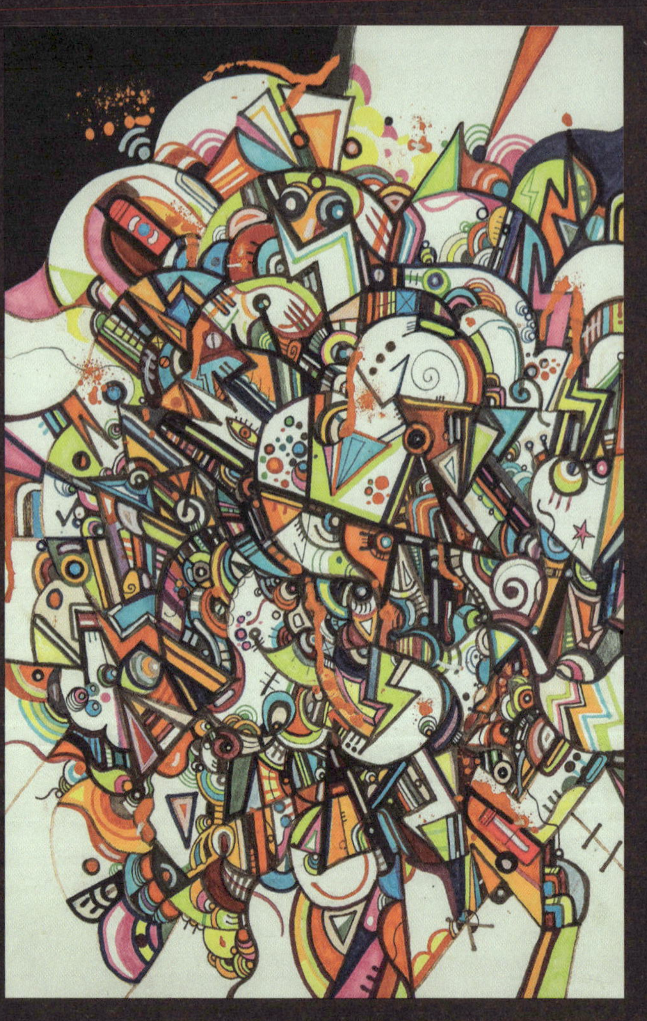

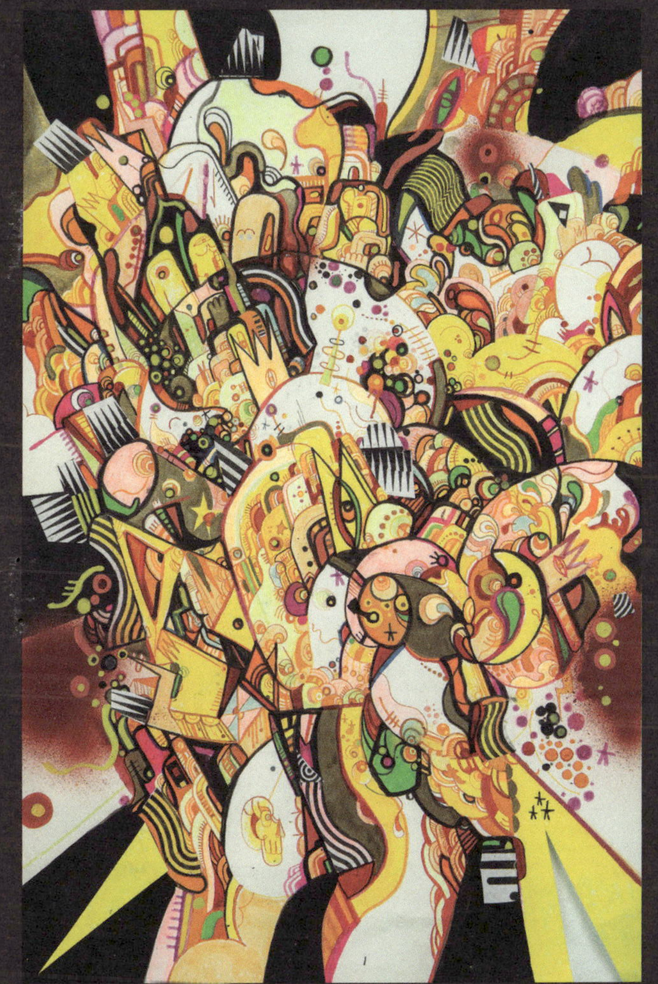

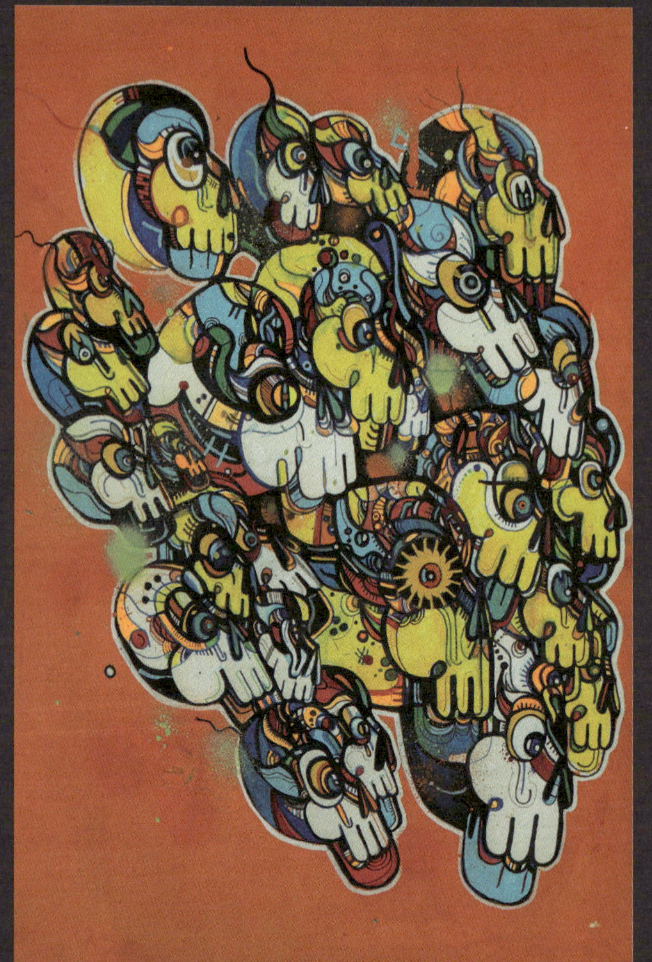

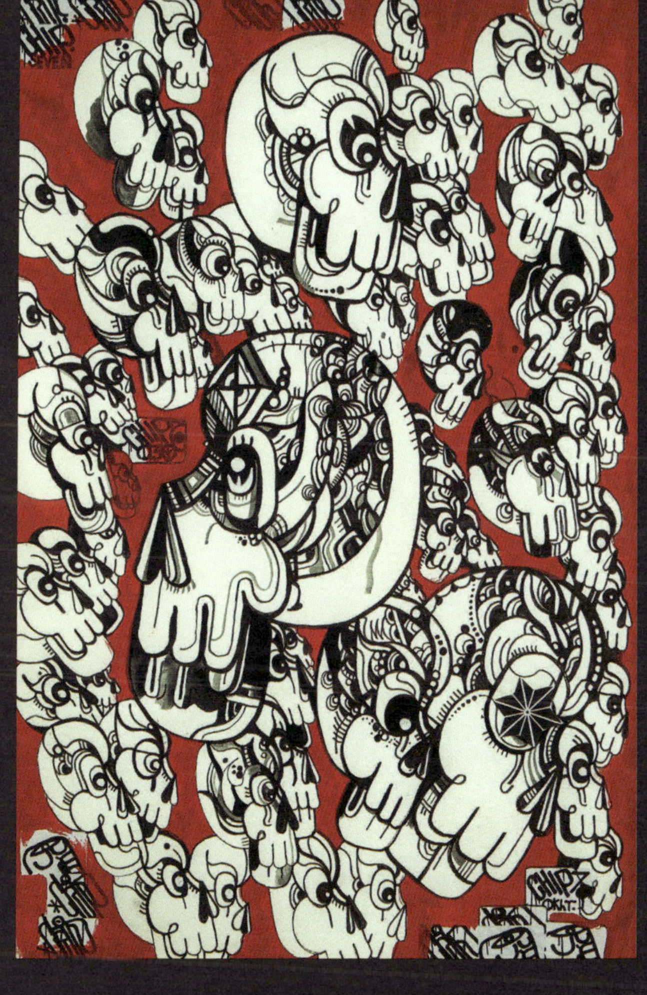
CHIP7

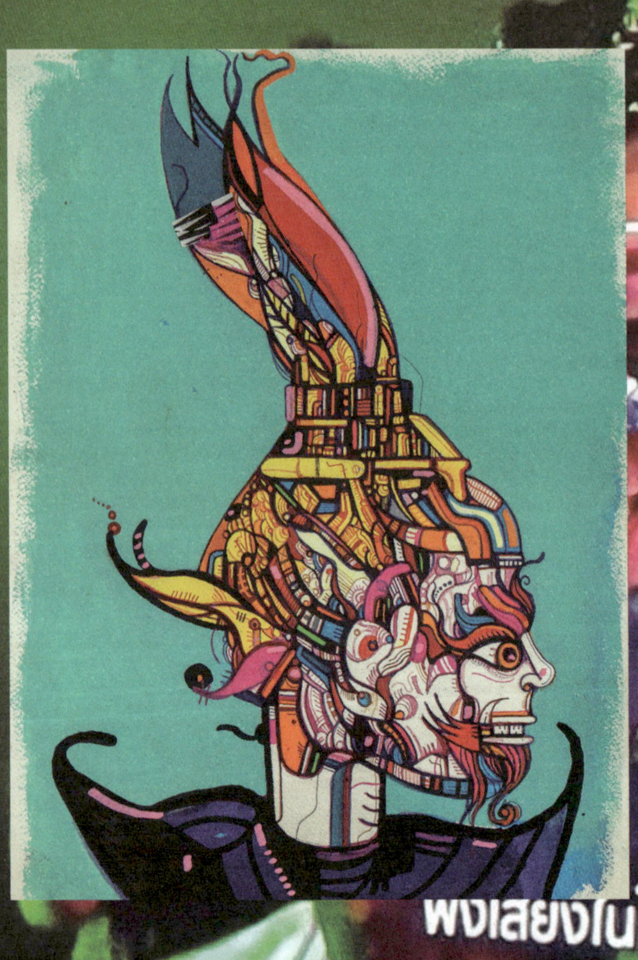
พงเสียงในใจ

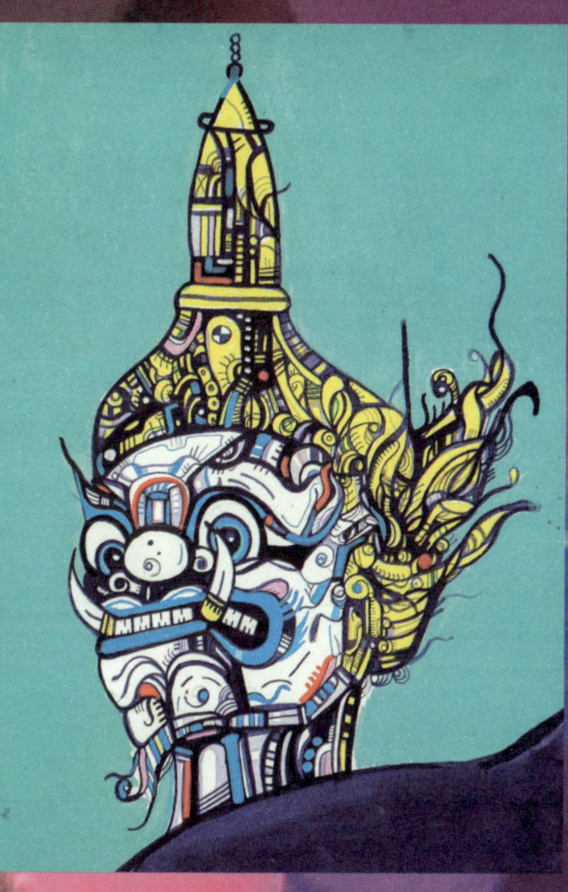

สังคม

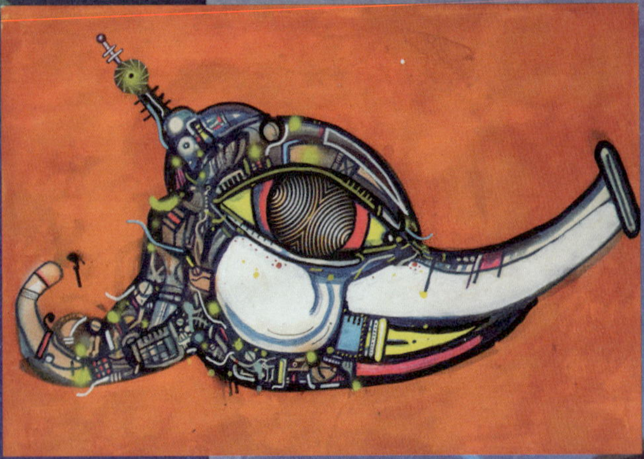

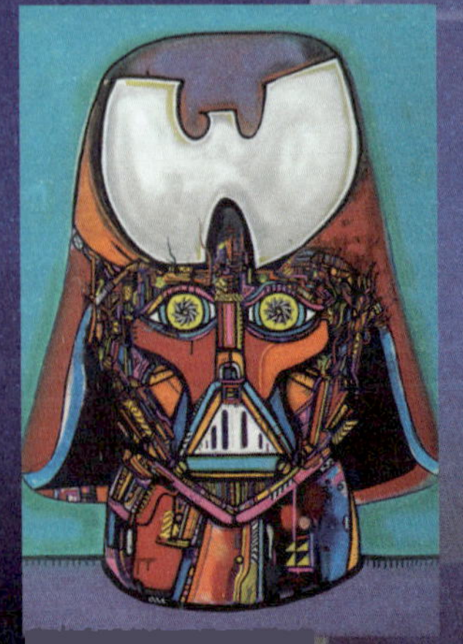

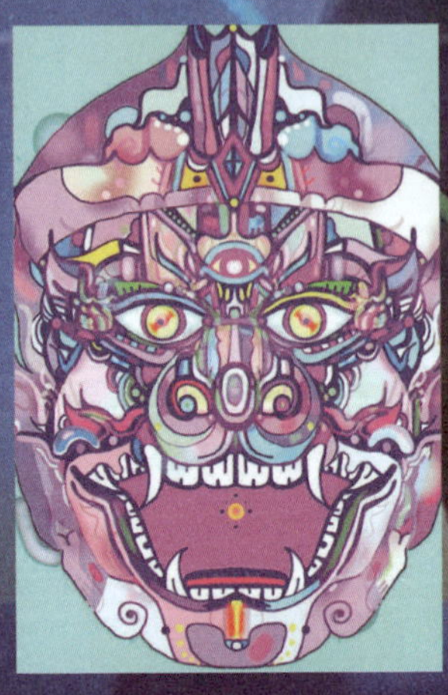

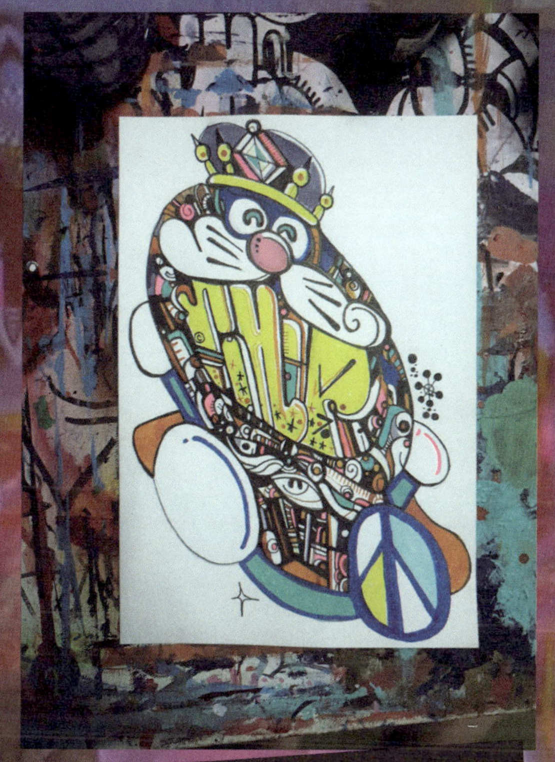

A Star flight round trip,
My nickname signed with drips,
It's Khun Nutt and Computer Chip

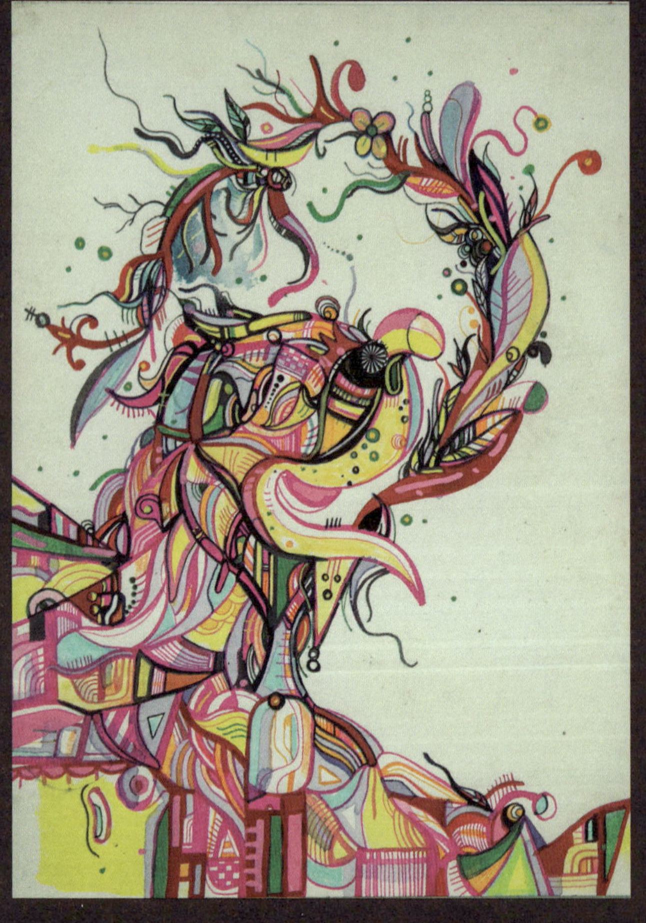

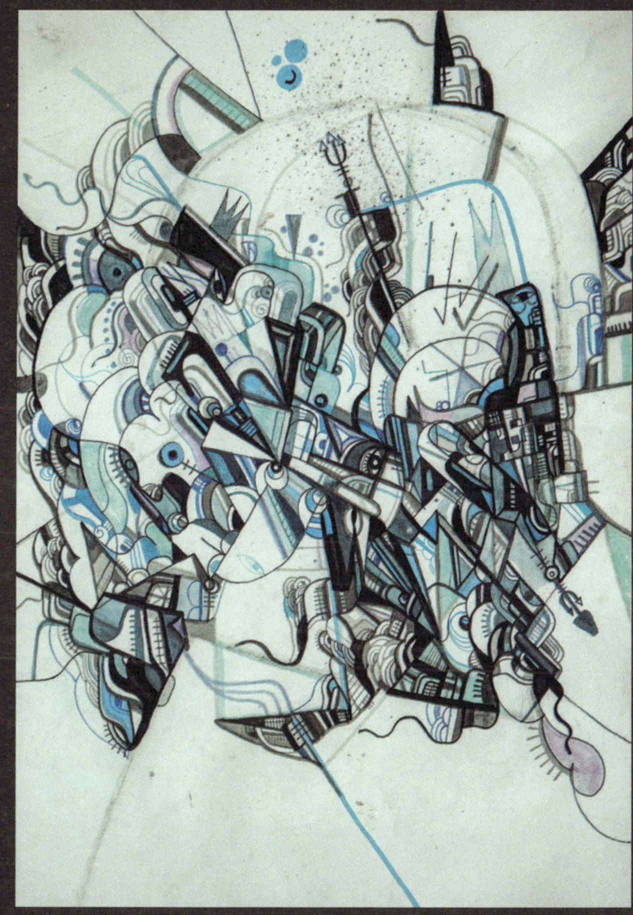

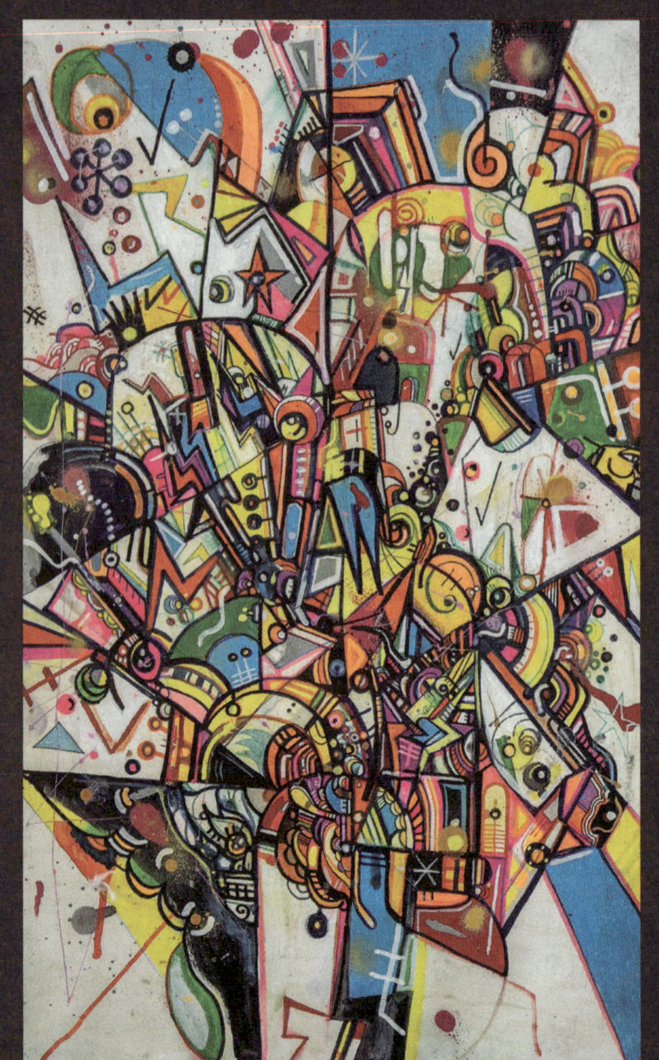

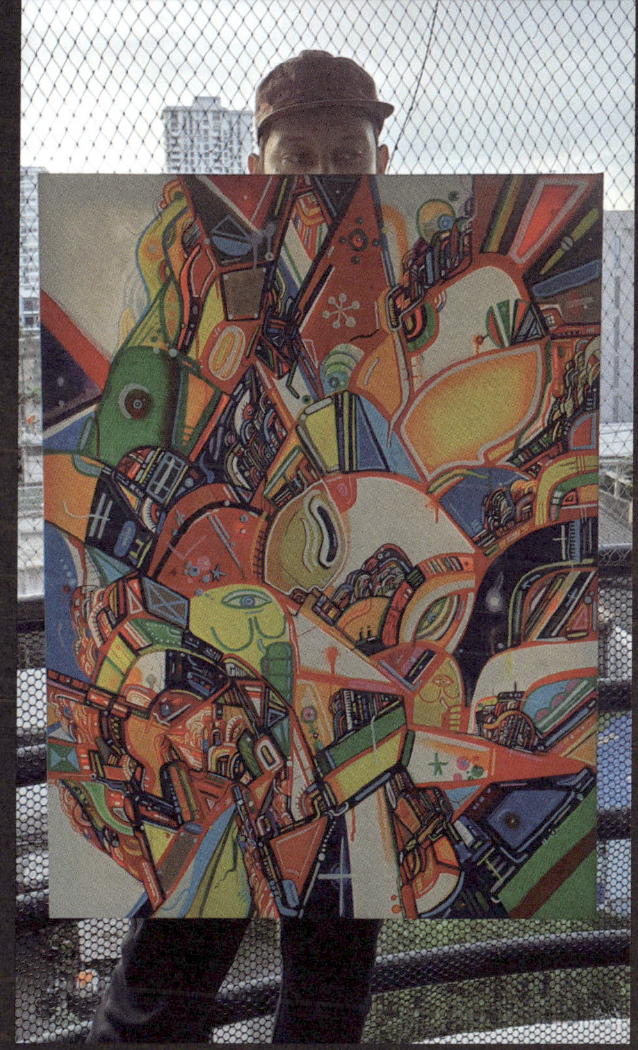

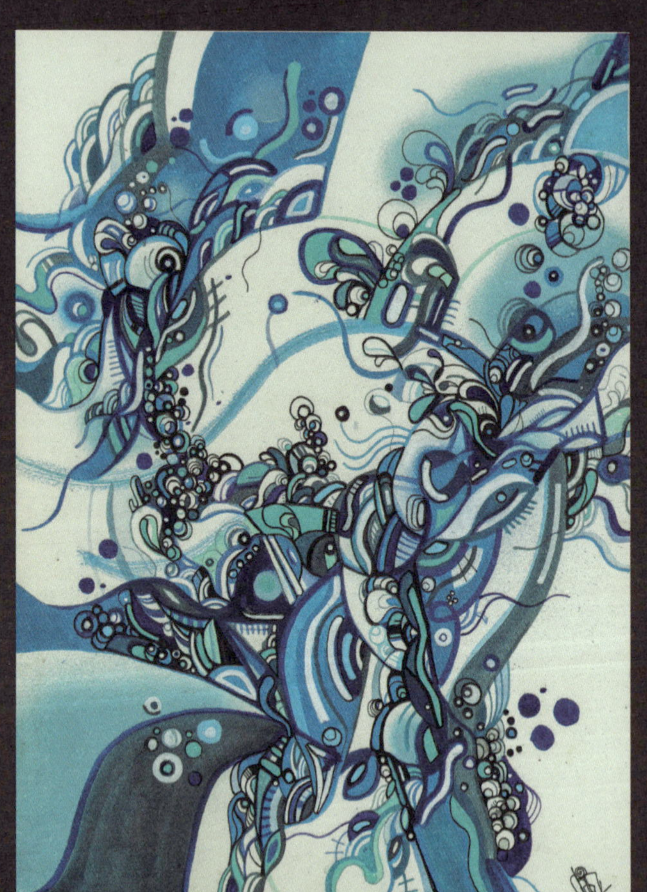

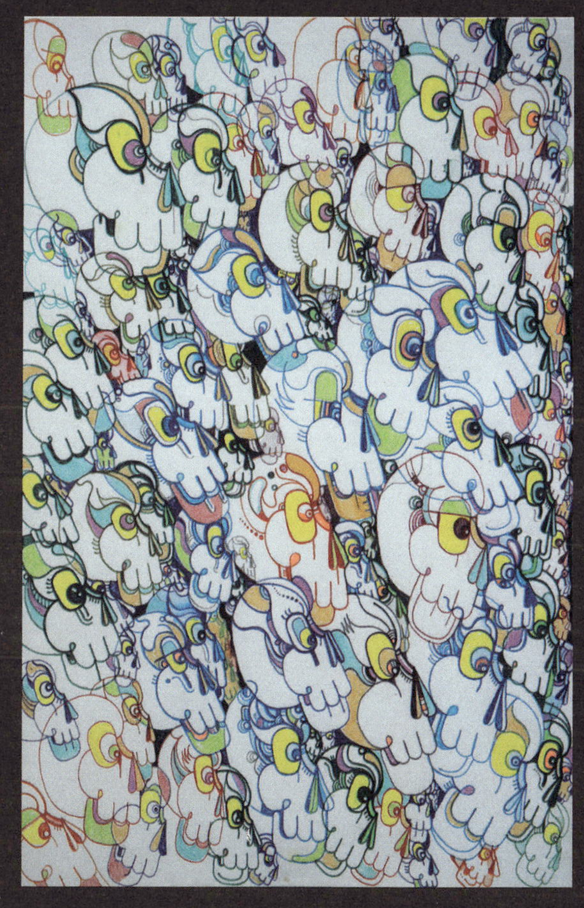

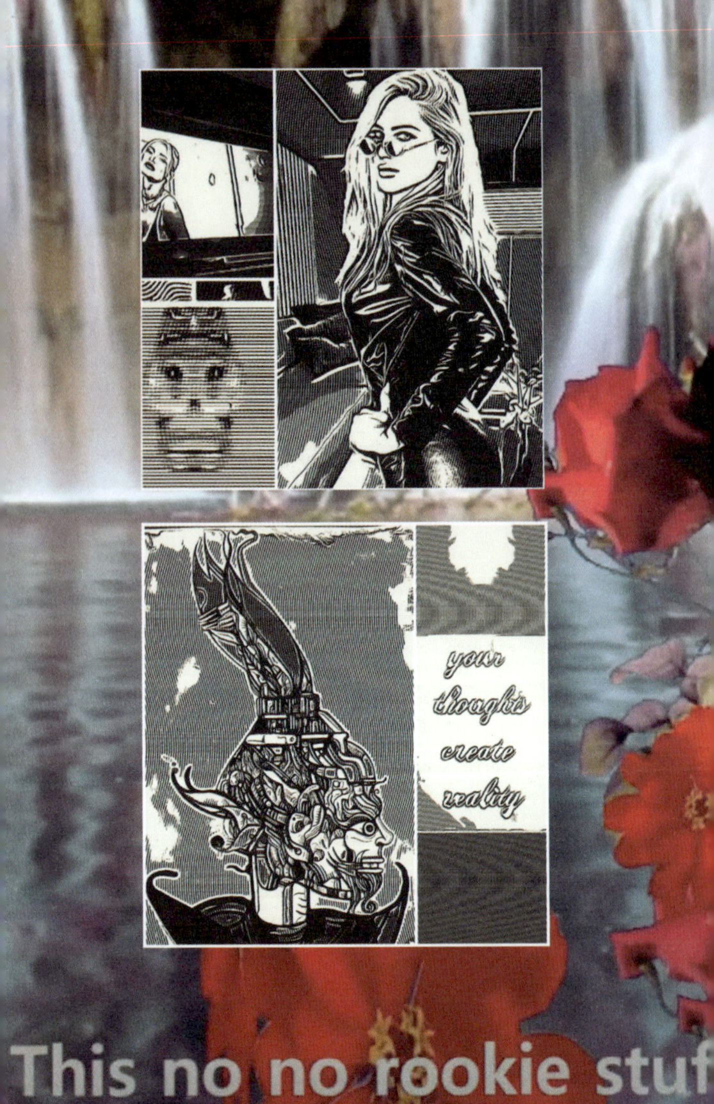
your
thoughts
create
reality
This no no rookie stuf

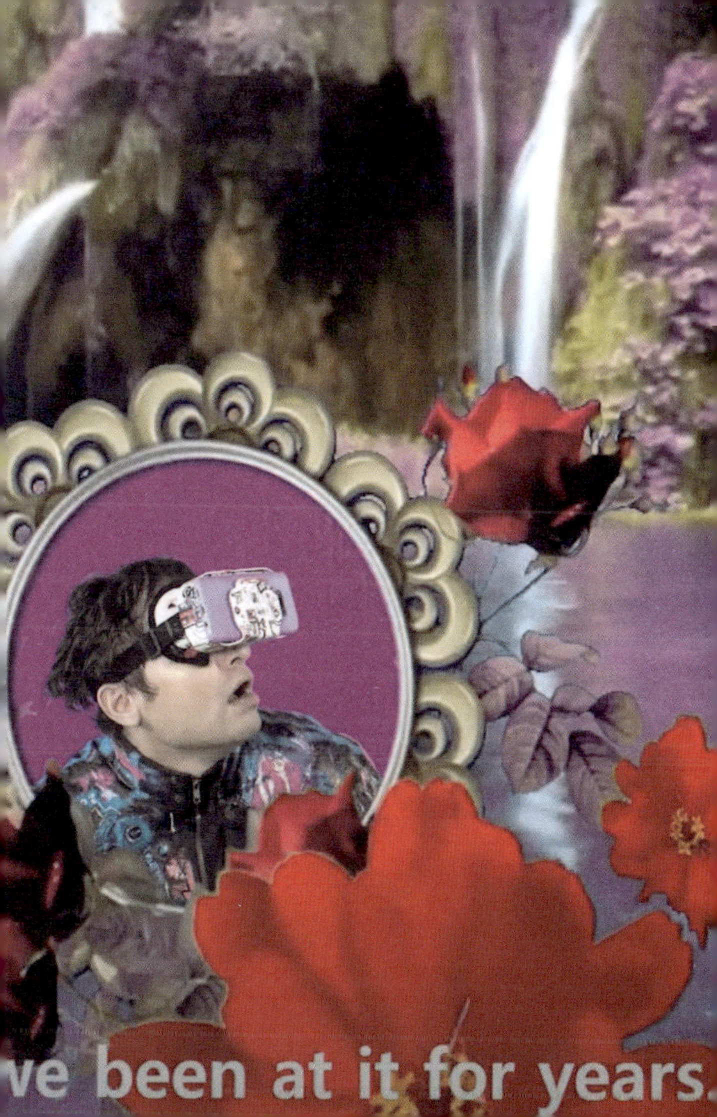
ve been at it for years.

In this adventure, from diapers to dentures
Drastic Times call for even more drastic measures
And that memory of her touching me
Remained my favourite pleasure

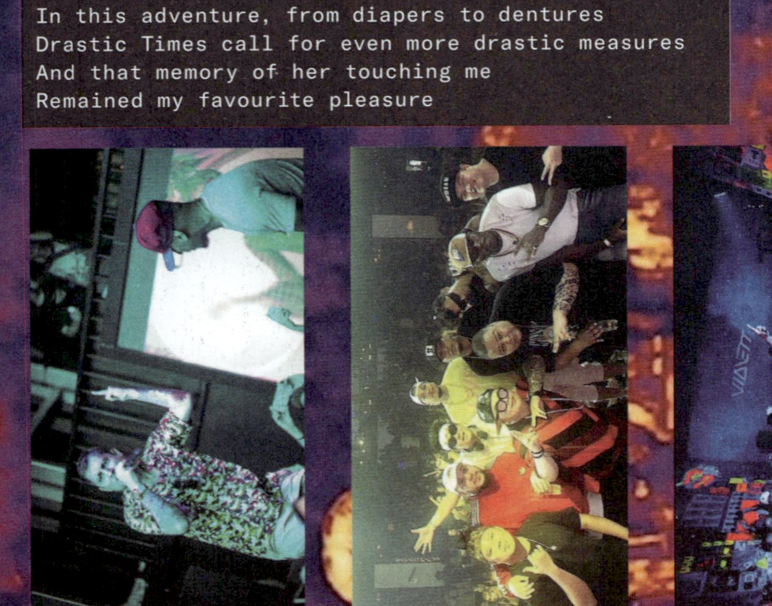

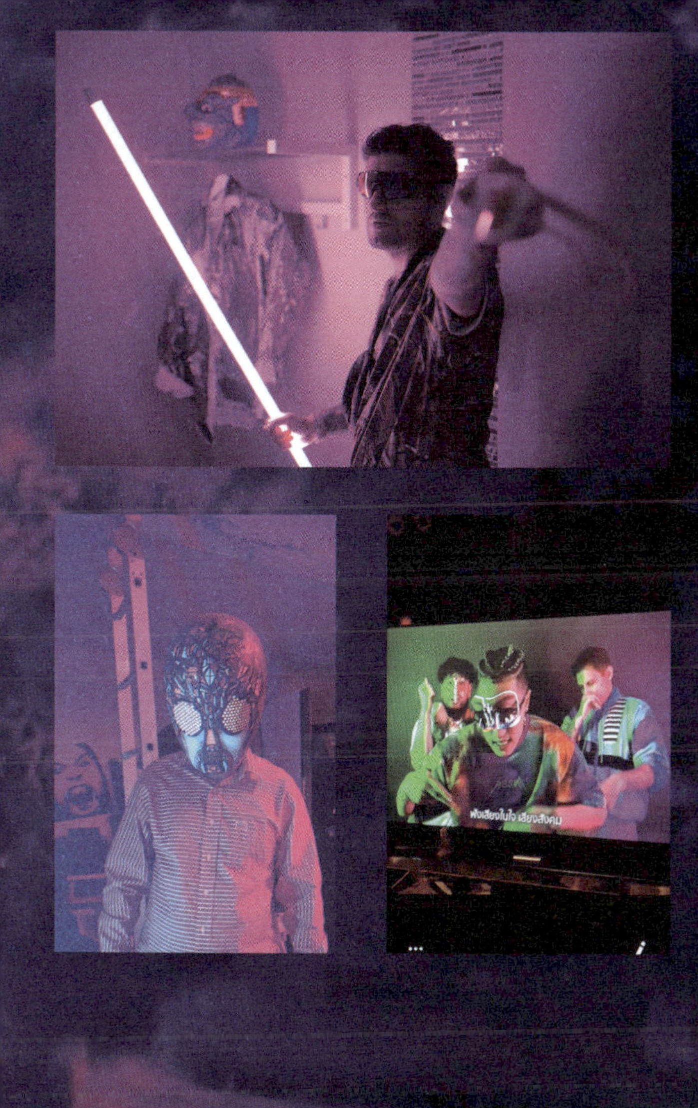
ฟังเสียงในใจ เสียงสังคม

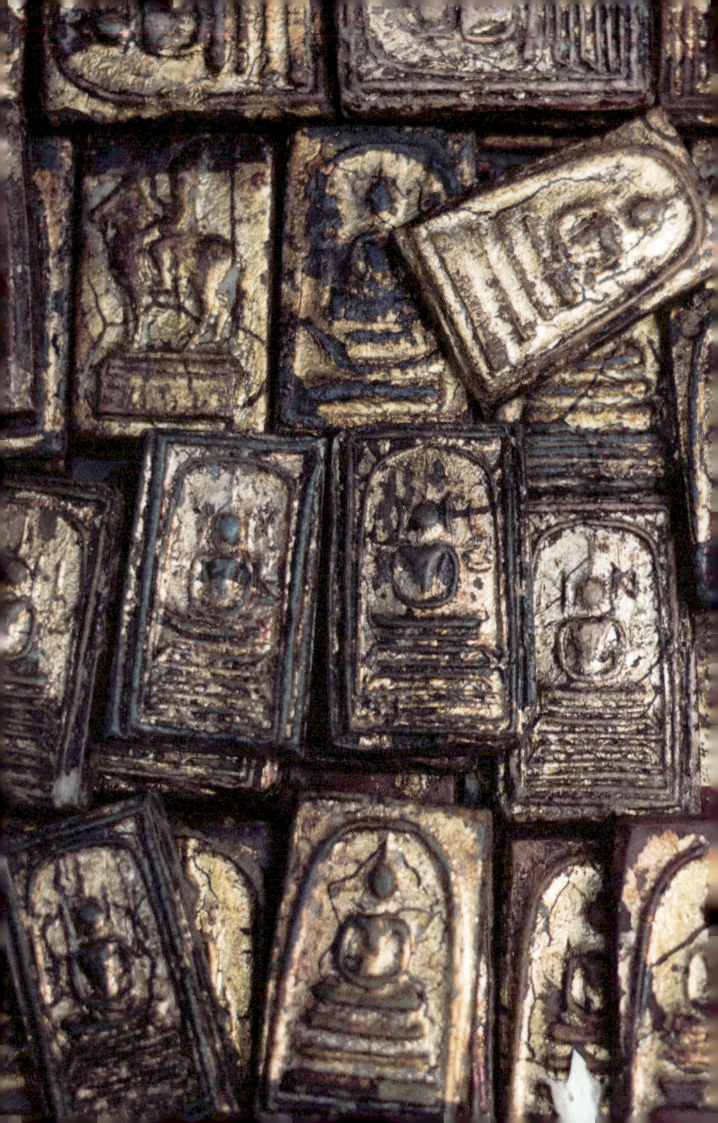

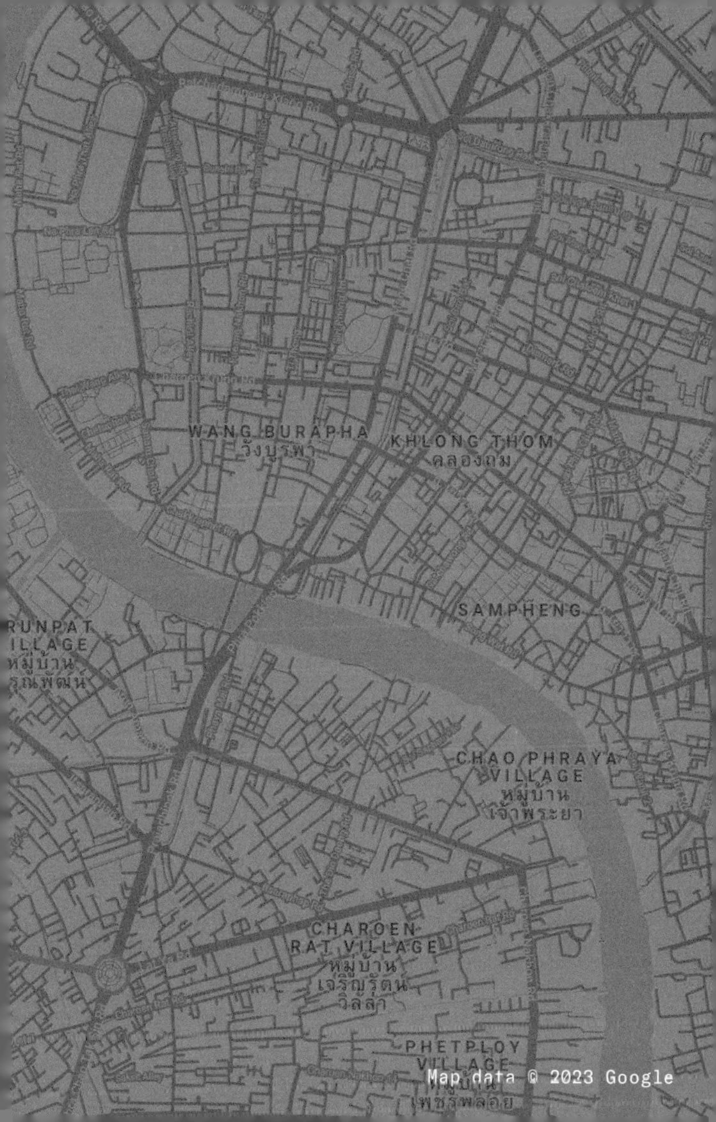
WANG BURAPHA
วังบูรพา
KHLONG THOM
คลองถม
SAMPHENG
RUNPAT
VILLAGE
หมู่บ้าน
รุณพัฒน์
CHAO PHRAYA
VILLAGE
หมู่บ้าน
เจ้าพระยา
CHAROEN
RAT VILLAGE
หมู่บ้าน
เจริญรัตน์
วิลล่า
PHETPLOY
VILLAGE
Map data © 2023 Google